LEVERAGING TENSION

**DON'T LET TENSION KNOCK
YOU OUT OF COMMISSION!**

Cover Art: Todd Bishop
Editor: Jaimie Jerome & Gina Bellomo

Leveraging Tension
ISBN: 978-0-359-63499-6
Copyright © 2019 by Todd R Bishop

**DEDICATED TO THE PASTORS WHO
LEAD WELL AND LEAD LONG!**

WHAT OTHERS ARE SAYING

"When God gives you a new position, there will always be opposition. *Leveraging Tension* is full of practical tools for growing through trials and adversity so that you can become the leader God destined you to be! Get ready to learn that there is no limit to where you can go relationally, emotionally, and organizationally when you are biblically set up for true success no matter what you face. So grateful to Todd for this book and its impact on the lives of leaders everywhere and at every level."

ED YOUNG
Senior Pastor – FELLOWSHIP CHURCH – Grapevine, TX

"Growing up, tension was a constant part of my life! After a while, you start to wonder, *"Am I just too screwed up for God to ever use me?"* (Lol) Pastor Todd teaches, how every bad thing that's happened to us can actually start working in our favor! In his new book, *"Leveraging Tension,"* Todd Bishop has *unleashed* another brilliant bit of wisdom. Don't just *live* with your pain... learn to *leverage it* for your own good! The tension we face has the power to *make us* or the power to *break us!* The choice is, totally, up to us!"

DAVID CRANK
Senior Pastor – FAITH CHURCH – St Louis, MO,
Royal Palm & West Palm Beach, FL

"It comes as no surprise that over 90% of American's claim to have stress in their lives. When stress is inevitable, how can we use those tense feelings productively? Todd Bishop brilliantly answers that question in *Leveraging Tension* by providing practical steps for any leader to follow. I've had the privilege of knowing Todd for a while now and I've always admired his ability to teach the teachers and lead the leaders. This book provides a fresh perspective for leveraging the pressures in our everyday lives. No matter your level of leadership, you will be blessed by *Leveraging Tension*."

CHRIS DURSO
Author – THE HEIST: How Grace Robs Us of our Shame

"*Leveraging Tension* helps leaders turn their tension into transformation. Practical, yet powerful truths that will inspire you to lead confidently."

CURT DEMOFF
Lead Pastor – BRIDGEWOOD CHURCH – Detroit, MI

"Any leader with great dreams is going to face great challenges and a leader who inspires others to dream great dreams will be surrounded by people who face great challenges. Thankfully, Todd Bishop teaches us how to leverage the tension of leadership challenges in his insightful new book, *Leveraging Tension*. This is a fun read with an important message, and you will be a better leader for having read it."

TERRY A. SMITH
Lead Pastor – THE LIFE CHRISTIAN CHURCH – Orange, NJ

"Levering Tension provides a fresh, practical and insightful approach in dealing with the unavoidable tension we face on a daily basis. It is rare a book can tackle the issue of tension in a biblical inspiring way, but Todd Bishop has managed to unpack this difficult, overlooked area of our lives. This is an important message in an era riddled with tension. Without tension, I highly recommend this book!"

DR. FERNANDO CABRERA
Lead Pastor – NEW LIFE CHURCH – Bronx, NY

"If you're looking to become a better leader then *Leveraging Tension* is a must read! Todd shares from his years of experience pastoring and church planting to help leaders gain the upper edge when dealing with the emotional and mental strains of leadership. In this book he gives great insight on leveraging tension from your past, present, and future to help you achieve your goals and walk in your destiny. *Leveraging Tension* will help you learn to build a bridge with the tension in your life instead of accepting the barriers it brings."

JEREMY MALLORY
Associate Pastor – GOSPEL LIGHTHOUSE – Hudson Falls, NY

"In his latest book, *Leveraging Tension*, Todd Bishop presents a compelling case for leveraging the unavoidable tensions that every leader eventually faces. Todd, with his tactical and practical leadership style challenges us to embrace and not just endure the tensions of leadership when they surface. *Leveraging Tension* is a must read that will ultimately leverage your leadership."

KEITH SHAW
Lead Pastor – SHIRLEY ASSEMBLY OF GOD – Shirley, NY

"Leveraging Tension' is a perfect resource to help navigate through tension in order to rendezvous to triumph. This book is not a simple prognosis as to the outcome of confronting tension. Rather, *Leveraging Tension* helps the reader diagnose tension by developing a healthier, more strategic perspective when experiencing pressure, struggles and difficulty. Since no one is immune to tension, every leader needs a resource that "Boosts the immune system" to help fight the urge to quit in the midst of opposition, *Leveraging Tension* is it."

KYLE WATKINS
Campus Pastor –AXIS CHURCH – Patchogue, NY

"Pastor Todd's passion for raising up leaders is seen on every page of this book. If you are a leader, you will experience tension; and the principles found in *Leveraging Tension* will set you up to succeed! I love what Pastor Todd said: "Too many leaders internalize instead of mobilize." This book WILL mobilize you to be a better leader."

KEITH INDOVINO
Lead Pastor – TRUTH COMMUNITY CHURCH – Flanders, NY

"Todd has written a must-read for anyone in any leadership position! He brings a fresh perspective on a topic ALL leaders face, yet seldom talk about or embrace. He has been a friend for over two decades, and I encourage you to get *Leveraging Tension* and learn from one of the best."

STEVE BELLAVIA
Lead Pastor – RELATE CHURCH – Virginia Beach, VA

"Every time Pastor Todd Bishop releases what's in his heart to empower people, those who are touched by his wisdom are made better. In *Leveraging Tension,* he upgrades our thinking and opens our hearts to accept the fact that our pain always positions us for a great purpose. His words in this book will open your eyes to see the beauty in what you thought was an ugly situation!"

MARCUS GILL
Lead Pastor – ENCOURAGERS CHURCH – St. Louis, MO
Pastor, Author – Marcus Gill International – Myrtle Beach, SC

CONTENTS

OPENING THOUGHT

In 2018 I was invited to encourage a group of pastors in the Bronx. I was given a subject to teach on, but no theme to focus on, and no suggestion to follow. Simply, "Whatever God lays on your heart, brother." I was torn between three talks I could have given in that moment but felt no internal directive. So, I did what any communicator would do. I gave the audience the option for which talk I should give.

The pastors voted.

I shared a teaching I called, "The Ministry of Tension." It seemed to resonate as multiple pastors approached me after and shared how they really needed that encouragement. I thought I was the only one who faced tension, struggle, and difficulty as a leader. Isn't that funny, how we think we are the "only one" until we open up and share. Then we find out we are not the only one. It almost seems like we keep silent about our challenges as though it is our rite of passage as a leader. We say things like, "Nobody understands." Or "You have no idea what it's like." But the reality is leaders know what leaders know! Every leader who has ever led anything knows what every other leader knows. Here's it is: *We all face tension.*

Well, at the end of the talk I shared with that group of pastors, one man came up to me and said, "Todd, I think I know what your next book should be." I said, "What are you thinking?" His response was quick, sharp, and serious. "Leveraging Tension, that's your next book." Wow, I never thought a 45-minute encouragement to pastors would be seen as a possible book, but Marcos Suazo saw what I did not see before I did. I pray that my thoughts and insights inspire you the same way it did for Marcos and that group of pastors in the Bronx.

Leveraging Tension exposes my heart and brings you deep into the stress that leaders experience. Every person faces tension. Whether you are a doctor, preacher, parent, teacher, politician, or whatever. You cannot escape it. But you must learn to leverage it.

Every employment decision, vision adjustment, business agenda, and leadership process has an element of tension. I pray that as you read my thoughts you would discover that God will always bring you through what life has brought you to. Keep going. Don't quit. Never give up. You are just getting started and God has a bigger plan and purpose for your life than you could ever imagine.

I desire to encourage you to never quit. Remember, hell fights the hardest those who God wants to take the highest! So, the enemy sends tension in our life to try and terminate us. But if we choose to see our tension as an opportunity then we it will only make us stronger!

As you read this book, I pray that you develop an inner strength as a leader, to overcome every obstacle, survive any setback, and be better after every battle. You don't have to cave after chaos.

You can rise above it. So, whether you are a stay-at-home mom, business owner, pastor, politician, barista, or city employee, this book will inspire you! Grab a cup of coffee, get on your back porch, and start reading today!

Don't let tension knock you out of commission.

Face it.

Embrace it.

Leverage it.

PART I

THE ANOINTING OF TENSION

Several years ago, I had a very dear friend say to me, "Todd, it seems like conflict follows you." At first, these words cut me to the bone (okay, not really but certainly adds dramatic effect, right?), but over the years, I have been able to process them a little. In this process, I have discovered that tension in life is actually healthy. Many people try and avoid it at all costs, but tension that is managed well creates opportunities for personal growth. So, Chad, thank you for sending me on this 15-year journey in order to write this book.

Paul is writing to the church in Corinth. He says, "There's an amazing door of opportunity standing wide open for me to minister here, even though there are many who oppose and stand against me" (1 Corinthians 16:9 - TPT). In essence, Paul was saying that opposition is part of the process. I know, it is the part that no one likes or enjoys, but regardless, it is a vital part of it.

Every single person faces tension. But the key to life is not found in staring it down but leveraging the tension you face. Marriage will cause tension. New parents will face tension. Broken homes will experience it. Sickness will cause tension. A new job has instant tension. Let's not forget the tension of losing your job. Whether becoming a CEO or leading a church, there will be opportunities for tension. You see, no one is immune to it. Tension is a part of our lives. Try and run from it and it will smack you right in the face.

Man, does that hurt.

Along this journey, I have come to define tension as an opportunity to allow opposition to grow your life. I learned very early in life that if you don't leverage your tension, someone or something else will manage it for you. Growth requires tension. The further your goal, the more intense the opposition. Resistance is part of life. If you don't understand that, you will live life disappointed. No one prays for difficulty nor should we, but difficulty will come. It may come in the way of a pink slip, a bad report, or a broken friendship, but difficulty does not have to define you. It can truly refine you.

Leaders must leverage tension all the time, from the moody employee who wears every emotion on his or her sleeve to the introvert who says nothing in a brainstorming session. It's part of the job. If you want to lead anything, expect tension. As a pastor, I experience it on a regular basis.

"The music is too loud."
"The smoke machines are unnecessary!"
"I don't like this _____ (*fill in your own blank*)."

I hear it all the time. The fact is, if you are not ready for tension, then you are not ready to lead.

IF YOU ARE NOT READY FOR TENSION, THEN YOU ARE NOT READY TO LEAD!

Here's what I have learned: You have to learn to embrace tension. I know, it sounds crazy, but embracing tension prepares you for what's next. Inside information – sometimes I change things just to create tension. It's true. People do not grow without it. So sometimes, as a leader, you will have to create tension that did not exist before! I guess you could say I have an anointing of tension! It's not a disease, it is a directive. Leaders who can leverage tension lead at a higher level, accomplish more than others, and set the standard for other leaders.

The truth is, everyone wants what someone else has, until they have to go through what someone else did.

Amen.

Mic drop.

Every leader I have ever examined who has excelled went through something to get to somewhere. I remember listening to a well-known pastor say, "Everyone wants a large church like mine, but no one wants my scars." That stuck in my mind because it is so true. We see the testimony, but we did not see the tests. We hear the message, but we did not watch them navigate their mess.

Tension is best seen under a microscope. You have to get close to see the details. The closer you get to people – leaders or not – you will quickly see how they handle tension. So, sip on your latte, curl up with a blanket, grab a bag of Doritos, and learn from the 15 years' worth of lessons from 'Tension Todd.'

GENESIS OF TENSION

I have seen blogs, read books, and heard messages claiming you don't have to be stressed, but the truth is stress and tension are part of life. Avoiding them keeps you stuck. Embracing them makes you depressed. Leveraging them makes you a leader! There is not a single person on the planet who lives with no stress. I don't care what someone says, preaches, posts, or writes, it does not exist. Tension is a part of life.

Tension comes from a variety of places. Have you ever had a tense conversation? I have. Usually it's my wife Mary saying, "Todd Richard ...." Just kidding, (but no, not really). Some of my biggest areas of growth from tension have come from *difficult conversations*. Let me be clear: I do not like those moments, but I need them.

A dear friend of mine, Alan Stein, used to meet me for lunch every other month or so before being promoted to Heaven in 2016. As an older, wiser, more experienced pastor than me, he would always ask, "What are you preaching on? What's your text? What is God saying?" Then we would talk. But then there were times when he would pull out his small, pocket-sized notebook and say, "Todd, do you believe this?" He would then share something I posted on social media or something he heard. Al would then tell me how it sounded, even if it wasn't what I meant. Those were some hard conversations. They were sometimes tense, but they caused me to grow. I miss those talks.

I also believe that *relationships* will always have tension. When Mary and I first were married in 2001, she had to adjust to becoming a pastor's wife. That was not easy. The long days and late nights were constant and demanding for a youth pastor in a vibrant church. Mary had the courage to create tension because she loved us. She had the tough conversations because she valued our relationship. It took me some time, but I choose Mary over ministry.

Another tension creator is our own *thoughts*. Oh man, I should write a book just about this. My thoughts are often all over the place. I literally live life in ADD-HD. What's that? "Attention Deficit Disorder in High Def." In fact, if they were giving diagnoses when I was a child, I would have definitely fit the bill. You see what just happened! Back to thoughts. My mind often creates my mood. If my thoughts are negative, my day will be negative. There is a constant wrestling match in all our mind.

The average person has about 60,000 thoughts per day and 48,000 of those are negative (Mayo Clinic). Are you kidding me? That will definitely create some tension. You might say to me, "I want to stay positive, but my mind leans negative." Yep, I have been there too. When a negative thought comes to mind, replace it with a positive statement. Each morning when I wake up, I go to the bathroom, look in the mirror, and say, "You are best looking person in this room." Fact is, I am the only person in the bathroom, but I start each day with a positive expression.

This one might be a no-brainer, but *conflict* creates tension. Conflict creates change and change creates growth! No one likes conflict. However, every person needs it in order to grow. I have never had a conflict that I faced confidently and said, "Yes! I am conflicted!" But on the other side of every conflict, I have found myself stronger, better, and more equipped. As a leader, you will always have conflict and if you don't, you are probably leading a sinking ship!

Let me be honest, I make quicker, more direct decisions when in the middle of conflict. Why? Because I have to. Without conflict, I don't feel the make-a-decision-right-away urgency. I can wait. But once there is a conflict, I must act.

> **I MAKE QUICKER, MORE DIRECT DECISIONS WHEN I AM IN THE MIDDLE OF CONFLICT!**

Your *health* can create tension. I am gluten-free, dairy-free, nut-free, and soy-free, so basically "flavor-free." That creates tension. I changed my diet several years ago. It was very difficult at first. I wrestled back and forth. Today, there is no struggle because I feel better than ever. At first there was tension, but now there is a trust. My diet works. I usually don't cheat. Sometimes I will on special occasions, but 99% of the time, I live by the pre-decision-thanks-to-tension I made based on my health.

As a leader, I love this one: *Leaders* create tension. Leaders who do not create conflict from time to time will not be leading much longer. If you have ever worked for a work-a-holic (my whole team just perked up), you know that they expect you to work as hard as them. Day off? Seriously! I may still text you or email you, because I am always working. The tension is whether or not you respond to them on your day off. If you do, you leveraged the tension. If you don't, the tension may be leveraging you. You have to make a choice.

Leaders leverage tension all the time. They may add an event to the calendar or remove a program that is working or even release a team member, but your leaders are leveraging the tensions all the time. They never stop.

Politics create tension.

Enough said.

EVERYTHING YOU ARE EXPERIENCING – GOOD OR BAD – IS SHAPING YOUR DESTINY!

Finally, I believe that *spiritual matters* create a tension. There is a tension between doing what is wrong and knowing what is right. There is a constant conflict between sin and righteousness. The world says, "Do whatever you want." God says, "Do what I have asked." Our society lives in this debate all the time. Instead of embracing the tension that spirituality or religion create, we marginalize it. We cast it to the side. We don't embrace it, we resist it.

I am sure you have heard it said, "If you want to start an argument, talk about politics or religion." Why is that? Because people have a hard time talking about the tension they are feeling in their heart. Whether you embrace religion or not, its concepts often fly in the face of modern culture!

No matter what we embrace or face, we must learn to leverage our tensions. They are part of life. You cannot avoid them if you want to grow as a person or especially as a leader.

A PLACE CALLED DIFFICULT

Bible story time. Elisha has been following his leader Elijah for about 8 years. Elisha watched Elijah do some pretty incredible things, but now it was time for Elijah to leave earth. He is about to take a chariot ride to Heaven. Elisha asks for a "double portion" of what Elijah had. Elijah tells him, "You have asked a difficult thing." Long story short, as Elijah is being taken up to Heaven, Elisha cries, "My father, my father." Elisha chose to leverage the tension of loss by asking for double the anointing his spiritual father had.

Ready for this? According to Scripture, Elisha performed 28 miracles, doubling the 14 miracles Elijah performed. That is insane. Elisha turned his difficulty into a divine destiny! Too many people today run around complaining about their problems instead of leveraging them. Everything that you face in this life can either make you or break you. The choice is really up to you!

As I speak with pastors across this region and nation, I have heart to heart conversation with many who are disappointed, discouraged, and even depressed. Pastoring is more than preaching to the crowds, standing on a stage, or playing golf every day. The reality is pastors are in the trenches of people's pain, loss, tragedy, and sins. It is not easy. Most pastors, like me, can feel overwhelmed. We have to learn to leverage the tension of people's pains or else those things will manage our lives. The same is true of every leader: if you don't manage life, life will manage you!

I guess it all comes down to one word: perspective. If you only live for the next 5 minutes, you will live life disappointed by it. But if you can live life with a larger scope, you will discover that everything you are experiencing – good or bad – is shaping your destiny! As a leader, perspective is one of your greatest assets. With it, you are better, smarter, and more capable. Without it, you make long-term decisions on short-term data.

My friend, Carl Lentz, Pastor of Hillsong Church New York, once said, "You can't control what comes to you; but you can control what comes through you." That is perspective. Paul, the Apostle, also had an incredible perspective on life. He knew that God had a plan and a purpose in every situation. In fact, he said, while in prison, "Everything that has happened to me here has helped to spread the Good News. For everyone here, including the whole palace guard, knows that I am in chains because of Christ. And _because of my imprisonment_, most of the believers here have gained confidence and boldly speak God's message without fear" (Philippians 1:12-14 - NLT, _emphasis mine_). Notice what Paul said, "… because of my imprisonment …" Are you seriously kidding me? Most of us will never live with that thought process! But Paul knew that there was a purpose for the prison. That's perspective.

If I am being really honest, I whine about my problems way too much. There are times when I get upset that things don't go my way and that usually happens when I lose my perspective. We will all face storms, difficulties and problems but never forget *that if God wasn't going to use it – He would never have allowed it*. Leverage what you face.

Every single pastor, leader, and person will find himself or herself in a place called difficult. Pitch a tent because it is temporary. Don't build a mansion in your misery. Leverage what you are going through!

I DON'T WANT IT

No one wants tension, but everyone needs it. It is a vital part of growth and life. It often comes from unexpected people and places. Here's the reality: if you are breathing, you will have tension. You cannot wish it all away. You shouldn't want to. As I look back on my life, I am now grateful for all that I went through. I was not thankful for it at the time I was going through it. But in order to leverage your tension, you must embrace what you face and find something to be grateful for each day.

Rewind to the beginning, creation! Adam and Eve were created in a perfect environment and yet they still made a dreadful mistake. They had no long-term history with God. Adam and Eve could not look back 20 years to see God's faithful hand. In the face of tension, they made a long-term decision on short-term data. We all know how that worked out!

You may not want the tension. You're probably not waking up each morning praying for it. But hear this loud and strong: tension will find you! So, leverage the tension you walk through. No matter what it is, always remember there is a purpose to the process.

I grew up in a multiple divorce, low-middle class home on the church pantry assistance program. We did not always have the funds to do what my friends were doing, but my mother (aka my childhood superhero) tried to make a way – even if that meant sacrificing her hair appointment or clothing purchase. I faced a lot of challenges growing up that created tension. You may not be able to identify with all of my struggles, but perhaps you might.

Contrary to what you may think, I was an introvert growing up (truth be told, I still am). I had to work hard at relationships – they never came natural to me. I was made fun of growing up. I never heard my father say (until decades later) that he was proud of me. It got so difficult that I attempted suicide in my basement because I thought life would be easier without me, something I held in my heart for years without ever telling anyone. So yes, I know about tension. I never wanted tension. But as Chad reminded me, conflict follows me, and it became something I chose to leverage.

One of the best decisions of my life was going into full-time, occupational ministry. I wanted to leverage all the pain I experienced growing up and help young people who grew up in similar situations that I did. I became a champion for teenagers for 14 years as a Youth Pastor. Today, I still lead with a younger mentality, wanting students especially to know that someone is in their corner, cheering them on. I will never know how many students I impacted over those years, but I hope one day I will fully know what a difference I made in their lives. You see, a lot of people will allow their pain to stop them. They will live life on pause, but at some point, you have to push through the pain to find the purpose! I heard Rick Warren once say, "God never wastes a hurt." That is so true, but I also know that we waste a lot of hurts. We live with the pain of regret, failure, difficulty, and abandonment. I say this respectfully; don't live with it, leverage it.

TENSION TIME

Look inside to see what changes can be made outside.

1. Where are you facing the most stretching?

2. What tension has caused you the greatest hurt?

3. What 'place called difficult' have you built a mansion instead of pitching a tent?

PAY ATTENTION

Have you ever thought, "What causes me the most stress or tension?" You see, identifying where your greatest pain comes from makes you prepared when it knocks at your door. No one ever likes to be blindsided. Anyone who knows me knows that I am not a huge fan of surprises. We were celebrating our churches 5-year anniversary. I planned out every detail – little did I know some members of our team felt like they should also celebrate my birthday at this event. Although their hearts were in the right place, I was not happy with the decision to hijack our church's fifth birthday. Why? It was a surprise!

I have learned that surprises cause me tension. I don't like not knowing! But now that I know that I have to know, everyone else knows to make sure I know. Makes sense, right? However, if you feel like surprising me with a million-dollar check, I will get over the surprise really quick. I think.

Recognizing what causes you tension is what psychologists call being 'self-aware.' I know what makes me tick, and what makes me get ticked off. One of the healthiest things you can ever do is have honest conversations with yourself. It's true. Leaders who excel often have inner dialogue. I am constantly having conversations in my head. Now, before you call the local therapist, hear me out. As I am speaking on a Sunday to our church, my eyes scan the audience. In my mind, I am processing, "Should I say this or not say this?" At the same time, I am also asking God to speak to my heart on what I should say in that moment. Every leader who is excelling will find they do something similar. I have spoken to business leaders who are about to give the biggest pitch of their life and they pump themselves up internally. Have you ever watched a pitcher's mouth just before they throw that strike? Watch their lips. It often looks like they are having a conversation in their mind.

Create a healthy inner conversation. Tell yourself what you are good at, where you can improve, and the difference you are making in someone's life. Talk to yourself. Go ahead and do it right now! Seriously, take an inventory of your skills, talents, and abilities. You are better than you think you are. Remind yourself of all that you have accomplished and what God has done in your life.

Leaders that fail often spend their time talking to everyone else and about everyone else. Oh man, I have met my share of complaining leaders. You can quickly find that people who talk to everyone about every problem they encounter are typically stalled in their life and leadership. As a pastor, I hear other pastors complaining about their church all the time. My response is typically, "If you don't like it, move on." True leaders see the good in everything. They don't ignore the negative, they just choose to look through it!

So, what causes you tension? Where do you feel the most friction in life? Marriage? Home? Children? Leadership?

THE STRUGGLE IS REAL

When you walk in the anointing of God on your life – there is nothing that can stop you from your destiny. Yes, you are one of the 6 billion people on earth, but you are the only one with your anointing! "I don't want this anointing of tension," you may be saying to yourself, but that tension is producing something in you. Don't run from it or avoid it. Embrace it.

I read this about a spider somewhere. Not sure if the words are exact (as I get older, I realize I forget more than I remember) but the details went something like this: "We've all seen how a spider spins a web in order to catch an insect. That web is filled with a sticky substance so that when an insect comes in contact with it, it not only gets tangled in the web, but it actually gets stuck. God made the spider so that its body releases a special oil that flows down to its legs. That way, it can just slide across the web while the other insects remain stuck."

THE ANOINTING ON YOUR LIFE WILL BREAK EVERYTHING THAT IS HOLDING YOU BACK!

The anointing will give you the ability to slide through worry, fear, difficulty, and discouragement. This ability that God has given you will cause you to leverage the tension you face. The special oil that flows from God will give you the ability to slide beyond your past failures, sins, relationships, and problems.

The Bible declares, "And it shall come to pass in that day, that his burden shall be taken away from off thy shoulder, and his yoke from off thy neck, and the yoke shall be destroyed because of the anointing" (Isaiah 10:27 - KJV). When you are living, walking, serving, and giving with the anointing that God has placed on you, things are broken off your life. Addictions. Habits. Sins. Struggles. Bad relationships. Financial difficulty. As you increase in your anointing, every negative thing is seen differently. You don't see how it is working against you. You actually begin to see how it is working for you!

Here's what I know about this anointing of tension – it will give you the strength to slide through what life has brought you to. I know it is easy to get overwhelmed. Trust me, I am there more than I would be willing to admit, but every season of tension has prepared me for a season of expansion. In the middle of it, the other side is very hard to see, but hear my heart today: God will not leave you where you are. The anointing on your life will break everything that is holding you back or keeping you down.

The struggles we all face are real, but you have an option with every challenge you face. Cave in or leverage it. I am choosing to grow every day in every way! That means I must identify what causes me the greatest stress. If I don't know the what, I will never figure out the how.

CHANGE IS UNAVOIDABLE

Change is always going to be a part of life. You will never be able to avoid it. No matter how comfortable we get, we can't become so comfortable that we avoid the things that tick us off and the things that make us tick. This requires honesty. We have to be honest about the changes we need to make – we have to pull the layers back and realize that the tension we are facing today will become our testimony tomorrow. Remember, it all begins with paying attention to what causes us tension.

If you are struggling in your marriage – the solution is not just to "go on vacation." That only pauses the problem. The solution is to determine what is causing the tension in your relationship, to talk it out, get the help you need, and make a change. If you are challenged by your health – the answer is not shoving another Twinkie in your mouth. It's to look at what area of your body needs help – weight, cholesterol, blood pressure – and make the changes that will help those. No matter what happens in life, we can expect change! Change is unavoidable.

"I don't like change" is one of the biggest misstatements I have ever heard. The truth is people only like making everyone else change. I know some of you are saying to yourselves, "Not me, I just want everything to stay the same." People that resist change in themselves only expect everyone else to change. In the famous words from Mulan: "No matter how hard the wind blows, the mountain does not bend to the wind." That's how most people live: No matter how good the change, I will not bend, adjust, or change.

Serving in the people business for nearly 25 years has given me a glimpse into human nature from a unique perspective. No one wants to change until they have to, but by the time they do, it is often too late. Those who radically change the culture around them are change agents. They are constantly evolving, and they are causing those around them to change.

Growth requires change. The more we are willing to change, the more we are able to grow. When we resist change, we are stalling out where we are. You are reading this right now because you want to leverage the challenges around you, right? That means you have to have more than a willingness to change, but a 'want to' change mentality. Change means creating improvements in every area of your life. It reveals your desire to learn, become, and develop. In order to grow, you must embrace change!

I love systems and structure. It is something that I truly embrace, but when those things begin to be adored rather than remain adjustable, I will stop my growth. For any leader to keep growing, they must embrace change.

Growth requires flexibility. I have to be honest: I am not that flexible when it comes to stretching. When I was a kid, I had a much easier time touching my toes, but now that has become more challenging. The truth is, flexibility in life is lost with age. Have you ever had tried to change your grandparents or someone who is past 60 years old? All too often, it is an impossible task.

Change is not optional, but growth is. Every person makes choices every single day. Those choices reveal values. I love reading the Bible and praying. It is high on my value list. So, each day I make time, early in the morning, to spend time in prayer and reading. But then there are some days when the kids wake up early or I get an emergency phone call that requires my immediate attention and I have to come back to that prayer time later. I can't become so rigid that I don't leave room to adjust my life. If I want to keep growing as a person, leader, friend, I will have to remain flexible.

Growth requires honesty. We must learn to be honest. The Bible says, "Be honest in your evaluation of yourselves ..." (Romans 12:3). The truth is we all have things that we would like to change about our lives – it could be a habit or a job or something about our physique. I believe that most people would like to change to become more real or transparent in a lot of areas, but it first requires HONESTY. We have to be honest with ourselves.

We are not perfect, but too often we feel like we have to cover up who we are with masks, almost living in some plastic world with plastic people – none of which is real! Most people are convinced they need to live differently, but they just are not committed to it because they reject true, personal, honest evaluation.

I have to be honest: *I am not perfect.* In fact, I am far from it. I am truly a work in progress. I tell our church all the time that I am jacked-up, messed-up, and screwed-up. I am all kinds of up! I try to be honest with myself and others.

BE A PERSON OF THE NOW

We can't live in the past. The past is something that can't be altered or changed. We have to live in the now - today. One of the biggest challenges of change is focusing on what used to be. We can all get stuck there pretty quickly!

"I remember when I scored the winning touchdown ..."

"I remember when I closed the million-dollar deal ..."

"I remember when I got divorced ..."

"I remember when ..."

When we live in the past, we limit our potential! That's why we have to constantly move forward and toward our future in Christ. Scripture declares, "**Forgetting** the past and **looking forward** to what lies ahead ..." (Philippians 3:13 – NLT). Basically, Paul is telling the church at Philippi to be "people of the now." What are you doing today? What are you accomplishing now? Live in today!!!!

CHANGE IS NOT OPTIONAL, BUT GROWTH IS!

You see, eventually we have to move forward. It's the only way to the change! In fact, I believe it's the only way to live! Don't stay in the past. God has too much more in store for your life in the future! Identify what causes your tension and then leverage it!

Refuse to focus on your past failures or mistakes. Choose to look to the future because that's where life is truly found! Don't get stuck in memorized images but create some new memories today! It is very easy for leaders to focus on what "used to be" or "how we used to do it." You are not living in your yesterday; you are leading today! Today is a gift. That's why it's called the present.

People who live in yesterday will not lead long today. True leadership requires adaptation. Adaptation is the "state of adjusting." Each individual has to pay attention to every detail of his or her life. The only way you will be able to make the necessary changes while you are embracing your tension is via adaptation.

PEOPLE WHO LIVE IN YESTERDAY WILL NOT LEAD VERY LONG!

For many years I was living in the tension of my past. No one else was. Just me. I allowed it to affect every area of my life. The problem with most people and leaders is that while every other person has passed the past, they stay stuck there. How does that happen? They can base present decisions on past difficulties (which is not always a bad thing but can be). People who live in the past are always talking about how it used to be or what they used to do.

Choose to live in today. Don't focus on the past but don't force the future either. Enjoy today. Leverage the tension you are in!

RESPOND, DON'T REACT

I love the story in the Bible about *Josiah*. He is a young leader, only 8 years old – believe it or not – and the King of Judah. The Bible says in 2 Kings 22 that he "did what was pleasing in the Lord's sight" and "did not turn away from doing what was right." The leaders of Judah discover God's law and they realize that they have not been completely obeying it. This young king tears his clothes and weeps in repentance. God responds, "Because your heart was responsive and you humbled yourself before the Lord ... because you tore your clothes and wept in my presence, I also have heard you ..." (2 Kings 22:19 - NIV). Josiah changed Judah. He was able to do that because he had a responsive heart to God. How's your heart? Leveraging tension is really a heart issue.

So many people have non-responsive hearts – they can feel God speak to them, but then they do nothing after that! God says clean up your mouth – we say, "Yes God, but we'll get to it later." God says forgive that person – we say, "I will eventually – don't you know what they did to me?" God says let go of the past – we say, "I can't. It's all I got." God says walk away from that relationship – we say, "I know they are not a Christian, but I can convert her." You see, so often we have hearts to hear – but when God speaks, it goes in one ear and out the other. We never, ever change. We don't have a responsive heart!

Sadly, I also believe there are leaders with non-responsive hearts. They do not see their own blind spots. They make very little adjustments. One of the healthiest things I have ever done as a leader is to pay attention to what causes me tension. This allows me to respond to it, instead of reacting to it! I am honest about it. I let our staff know. My wife, Mary, definitely knows.

If someone is driving distracted, say on their cell phone or talking to someone in the car and they get into an accident, what was the cause? The cell phone? The other person? No, the one who stopped paying attention! When we as leaders don't pay attention to what causes us tension, we will get into leadership wrecks. We can destroy businesses, relationships, staff members, and ourselves.

Here's a small piece of advice: Ask the closest person to you what they feel causes you the most tension. It may be one of the hardest answers you will hear, but the person that knows you best loves you most and they will give you the most accurate feedback.

TENSION TIME

Look inside to see what changes can be made outside.

1. What encouragement do you need to hear and tell yourself?

2. How flexible are you in life and leadership? Why or why not?

3. Have you been reacting or responding to your tension?

THE TENSION OF GROWTH

Allow me to deflate your leadership bubble: growth doesn't happen in a day. It happens daily. Each day you are moving toward your destiny! Too many young leaders want to achieve greatness overnight but hear me: *there are no shortcuts to success*. None. Leaders who live by shortcuts will die by their addiction to them.

When I was in Bible college, I thought that everything would just come naturally to me because I was called to lead. The problem was that no one taught me that tension was good. Let me clear the air: tension does not always feel good, but it can be for your good! I believe that we grow better and faster during difficulty. It is so easy to put your life on cruise control when everything is going "perfect" but then add some struggle and you it will force you to grow.

Do you remember how you learned how to swim? I do. It was at the Buffalo Christian Club. It was a converted YMCA. They had the typical "Y" pool. I had no idea how to swim, but the instructor pushed me into the deep end. Do you know what happened? I learned how to swim real quick. Why? I had no other option! It felt like swim or die at that moment! I am sure someone would have jumped in to rescue me. I hope {gulp}.

It seems to me that there are many who want things handed to them, but I have learned that hard work and problem solving are critical for leadership growth. Tension creates growth. Leaders who run from tension are really running from their potential. Leaders are not called to be resistant but resilient! True leaders know the value of bouncing back. I know leaders who bounced back bigger and better than ever after facing a major problem.

LEADERS WHO RUN FROM TENSION ARE REALLY RUNNING FROM THEIR POTENTIAL!

Mary and I have some very dear friends who, during the recession of 2007, both lost their jobs. Can you imagine how difficult that must have been? But did they complain? No! They made life adjustments. In fact, they started their own company. It took off in ways they could have never imagined. Their income went to another level. They purchased a multi-million-dollar home and then another. You see, they did not allow their set-back to become their saga. They learned from the difficulty and stepped into their destiny.

Every leader I have ever met has faced pain, difficulty, and challenge. No one is immune to it. Whether you run a Fortune 500 company, lead a small business, pastor a church, work at Taco Hell (I mean, Taco Bell), or are a stay at home mom, there will always be tension. Tension is part of marriage, ministry, management, and movement! Don't run from it, grow through it!

PATIENT IN THE PRESSURE

I have a million dreams and ideas, more than I could ever pen. Most of them I am constantly working on. The challenge is I get stuck on not seeing results right away. When Mary and I first started our church, we prayed for an explosion of growth. That did not happen. The first three years were extremely difficult. There were many times when it would have been easier to just quit, but we did not. During that season of ministry, I developed a personal mantra: *Be patient in the process.* It helped me through some very difficult seasons. I just kept thinking, "Todd, stay patient. God will get you to where He wants you to be." See! Even then I was talking to myself! I was really putting that principle we spoke about earlier into practice.

The Bible declares, "Rejoice in our confident hope. Be patient in trouble and keep on praying" (Romans 12:12 - NLT). Notice, patience is wedged between hope and prayer. Hope is the birthing of a dream, patience is the hard work of the dream, and prayer is the only thing that brings them together. In order to lead long you need all three of these ingredients. I don't care whether you are religious or not, prayer is a vital key in this process. Every person prays in some way!

Eleven years ago when we began Church Unleashed, we prayed a million prayers. The start of our church was not very glamorous. It was hard to attract people, pay bills, and stay motivated. We knew God called us and even though we knew that, we still faced challenges. At times it felt overwhelming. A few years ago, Mary said, "I am so glad it was not easy in the beginning because it taught us to depend on God and trust Him. Plus, I appreciate where we are now even more." Wow. That's called being patient in the process.

I love this passage of Scripture: "Patient endurance is what you need now, so that you will continue to do God's will. Then you will *receive all that He has promised*" (Hebrews 10:36 – NLT, *emphasis mine*). All of us need a little patience but that often comes on the backside of tension. Did you catch the promise in this passage? It's an IF-THEN statement:

- **IF** you endure …
- And **IF** you do God's Will…
- ***THEN*** you receive all that He has promised!

So many people go through so many things but give up right in the middle of the challenge. Here's what I believe: *God has a promise on the other side of your problem.* Keep on keeping on. Hold on to hope. Never surrender and don't ever quit.

Patience is one of the critical characteristics of leadership. Leaders that are not patient lead by pressure instead of purpose. I have discovered that any leader who moves by pressure will lose their way very quickly! Pressure can come from anywhere.

Pressure comes from people. This is the easy one. I heard a leader say one time, "My job would be great if I did not have to deal with people." The only problem is that leadership is all about people! All types of relationships will have pressure. None are pressure-free!

Have you ever had a person in your life say, "I am just playing the devil's advocate?" I hate that expression. Yes, I am a pastor so anytime someone gets on the enemy's side I get angry. I mean, something in me says, "Why would you ever want to be on the losing team?" People use that expression to poke holes in an idea, program, or concept. But, I had this one person in my life who used that expression every time they disagreed with anything I was doing. "I am just playing the devil's advocate." Then they would add to it, "I am just looking out for you." Every time they said that, in my mind I would respond, "You are a child of the devil." Not really, but, yes, really. Needless to say, that person no longer has a voice in my life.

Pressure comes from problems. This one makes all the sense in the world. Once again, an easy one. That's why we, as leaders, must learn to manage our problems. We will never be able to eliminate them, but we must learn the lessons we need to from every problem we face.

AS A LEADER, WE HAVE TO SEE WHAT OTHERS CANNOT SEE!

After nearly 25 years of full-time pastoring, I have faced many challenges. Financial, emotional, relational, and physical difficulties are part of the leadership package. No one tells you about them when you first start out but hear me loud and clear: If you want to lead, be ready for problems. They are part of life and they are part of leadership. With problems come pressure.

Pressure comes from perspective. This is the big one. Just because you have your perspective, does not make it right. How you see an issue or address a challenge can add tremendous tension. If you fail to have the right perspective on anything you experience, you will add more pressure than required.

Perspective requires strong vision. As a leader, we have to be able to see what others cannot see and see it from the right angle. Seeing something and seeing it clearly are very different. We must be able to view everything through the perspective of patience. Here's why: without patience, you will never experience your purpose.

I CAN'T GROW HERE

One of the biggest barriers to personal growth is not place, but chase. You can grow anywhere if you want to. How hard do you run after growth? Are you reading books, listening to podcasts, reading blogs, or rubbing shoulders with influential people? You can grow anywhere. Don't let your environment be your excuse. Every leader will find themselves in negative environments. You may not be able to choose what happens to you, but you do get to choose how you respond to what happens to you!

There are many people who blame their today on the pain of yesterday. Now, I am not undermining what people go through, but blame keeps you the same. Every person must own their response to life – good and bad. You can *go* through life or you can ***grow*** through life. The choice is fully yours!

Don't compare your life to someone's social media highlight reel. Every person puts their best out there, but the reality is we all have pains in our past and problems in our lives. There are days I fight the thoughts of "If I had their money" or "If I knew their friends" or "If I possessed their skills." Regardless of thoughts, growing leaders will find ways to excel even in the hard places.

Leaders must learn to grow anywhere. Not every season we face will be positive and uplifting. Some are going to be painful. Some will push you to the edge of sanity but stop making the excuse that "I can't grow here." You can grow anywhere!

DON'T COMPARE YOUR LIFE TO SOMEONE'S SOCIAL MEDIA HIGHLIGHT REEL!

Growing up in a single parent home with multiple divorces, I experienced my share of difficulty! None more than my mother did, but still, it had a huge impact on my life. All the struggle I grew up with influenced how I view life and how I respond to people. I am a hard-worker because I watched my mother work hard to make sure there was food on the table, clothes on our back, and a roof over our heads. I am a faithful husband and father because I watched firsthand the pain of divorce. Not just once, or twice, but three times. I focus on hospitality because I was in multiple schools and was always the 'new' kid. Everything that I experienced groomed, shaped, and directed me.

Sometimes you and I are paralyzed by procrastination. We hide behind the idea of "someday." Someday I'll ask her out. Someday I'll apply for that new job. Someday I'll volunteer at church. Someday I'll have that difficult conversation. Someday I'll start to really read the Bible. Someday I'll start saving money. Someday I'll take time to pray.

Someday … someday … someday … is the one day that never arrives! And it starts because people think that they can't grow where they are. Don't believe that lie! Yes, you can!

The lazy drive me crazy! I have a hard time dealing with lazy, under-achieving, over-expecting leaders. There I said it. It's true. I work hard. I don't blame my past for my present. I won't make excuses for my life. We must work hard for the life we want or the leadership we crave. We cannot keep blaming our past for where we are. At some point, we must pass our past.

I was serving in one of my earliest pastoral positions. It was one of the most challenging seasons of my ministry. I questioned my calling. I was so discouraged. Why? Because the church board there cut my salary in half – two times! I was cursed out by one board members and was constantly being demeaned because I was young. But I learned a lot and grew a lot in that 9-month period. I learned that ministry is difficult, not every leader is good, and people can sometimes suck (wait for it) the life out of you! Seriously, there were so many lessons I learned. God taught me the value of persistence, integrity, and consistency. I discovered that I had gifts I did not know I had. It was in the fire I was refined and in that hard place I grew.

WHAT GOT YOU HERE

When Mary and I began our church ten years ago we learned one of the hardest leadership lessons: *Only those who grow with you will be able to go with you.* I wish that every single person who started this journey with us was still here. Many are, but not everyone. At first this was painful because I thought it was us. The difference between us now and us then is that we are not the same. We have grown in more ways than we expected. But what got us to where we are today may not be what we need to take our lives to the next level. It is all a matter of constantly evaluating our personal growth systems.

Personal growth systems will push you to increase your leadership! I have tried to maintain 6 personal growth systems. They are not about what I do as much as how they make me who I am. Here are the systems I am always tweaking: Family, Prayer, Reading, Structure/Schedule, Rest/Sabbath and Friendships. I am always working on making sure these systems are healthy. I do not get them right all the time, but I work hard at managing them. As a leader, it is critical to set up some systems that will help you grow.

LIVING OUT SOMONE ELSE'S DREAM IS A DANGEROUS DETOUR!

You will never grow by accident! How true is that? You will never get to your destination without a plan. I remember hearing this statement in a sermon many years ago: "A failure to plan is a plan to fail." If you are a CEO, what systems do you need to increase your bottom line? If you are a superintendent, what systems will help productivity in your teachers and administration? If you are a pastor, what systems will you need to develop to impact more people in your community? Every organization, business, and church need healthy systems in order to grow! As I evaluate my growth systems, I know I have to keep the following in mind:

Firstly, growth comes because we avoid dangerous detours. Over the years I have watched many of my friends make unwise choices that have led to moral failures. So, I am constantly guarding my eyes and heart from sin, wrong influences, poor decisions, repeated temptations and even someone else's vision. When we get off track, we can miss out on our potential.

Living out someone else's dream is a dangerous detour. That is the dead end of destiny! Live for your purpose. Choose to discover the design God has for your life and leadership. Watch out for the detours that will destroy your life.

Secondly, if you don't set your standards, someone will set them for you. Leaders truly don't get stuck following. They emerge. They rise higher. They set the pace for every other person. They are not settlers. They are pioneers. If you want to raise your leadership, be a trendsetter, raise others up, be the model everyone else wants to be, blaze new trails and step into the unchartered territory.

And lastly, don't ever look back. You are never going to do everything perfectly, but you have to move on from past mistakes if you are going to raise your leadership. Always press forward. Don't repeat the past – use it to learn and grow.

I have made the commitment to live life with no regrets. I never want to say, "We should have," or "We could have." I want to say, "We did" or at least, "We tried." In order to grow to the next level, you will need to do things you have never done before. Experimentation is one of the foundations to growth.

The only way that you can become who God has wired you to be is to constantly grow. ***You don't just go to the next level – you grow to the next level***! A position will not grow you. People cannot fully grow you. Tension, pressure, problems. Those are the things that will grow you quicker. You see, the valley places create a tension that the victory places do not. Don't complain about the pain! You are getting stronger, smarter, and better!

TENSION TIME

Look inside to see what changes can be made outside.

1. What area of your life have you been waiting for growth instead of working toward growth?

2. Which area of your life are you the least patient? Why? What steps can you start taking to develop patience in that area?

3. Are there some new boundaries that you need to set for your life to keep your personal growth systems healthy? If so, list them.

EGGSHELLS AND BROKEN GLASS

I have worked with several people over the years and with that, I have dealt with personalities on every end of the spectrum. Some have been easy to work with and others have been extremely difficult. Still there are many in the middle. By far, the hardest people to work with, for, or alongside are those who make you feel like you are walking on eggshells. You know the person. You have to guard, watch, and worry about everything you say and do because it is going to be evaluated to death. These have made for some tense moments in the office.

People will drive you insane. I know that sounds harsh coming from a pastor, but it is oh so true. No matter what you say or do, people will see your actions or words through the lens of their own insecurity! These people, employees, friends, or family members will suck your emotional tank dry. You will be left with the air knocked out of your lungs and you will feel like you are walking on broken glass.

In spite of those types of people, God has called us to be compassionate, patient, and "slow to anger." I wish the Bible said we were called to frustration, impatience, and quick-tempers, but that is where the tension lives. Dealing with difficult people is just part of life and leadership and it makes doing what is right hard, but that is what we are called to do. It's the part that sucks at the time, but serves us over time!

There are a few people who come to mind when I think of difficult personalities. I'm sure you can think of a few too. They drive me to the edge of insanity. For some, it's not insecurity that drives them, it is arrogance. You walk on eggshells because they are going to correct everything you say, do, and think because they can do it better! At least, they think they can.

PEOPLE WILL DRIVE YOU INSANE!

As a pastor I have had to have difficult conversations with people. Some end up really amazing. Others I leave with more questions than answers. I remember one meeting I had with someone where they brought up things they disagreed with from years ago all the way to present time. It was hard to hear some of their 'opinions,' but I listened. It hurt because most seemed to be subtle character jabs, not constructive input. Toward the end of the conversation I simply said, "I am not sure I will ever be good enough to be your pastor." You see, this individual had always made others feel that they were better than anyone else. Not every 'eggshell' personality is insecure – some are just arrogant.

You have a choice to make: *Walk on eggshells or get out of the eggshell patch.* You do not have to stay in the same zone you are in. Leave the eggshell patch!

PUSH ME DOWN A HILL

Have you ever left a conversation feeling like, "Push me down the hill?" (Sometimes I would love to say instead, "Throw me off of a cliff," but that sounds too painful and almost certain death.) It is those moments where you feel all the emotion, hurt, pain, and burden of someone's life put on you! It is a tough spot to be in because you want to help, you really do. But sometimes people need more help than you can give them.

As a leader. You are called to serve people. However, you also have to recognize when an individual is doing more damage than they are worth to your organization. Once again, sounds harsh, but every leader knows that one "tick" personality will suck the life out of your workplace.

So, how do you respond?

Look in their eyes and say, "Push me down a hill."

I'm kidding, you can't do that. First, you must give people time and space. See if they are willing and able to adjust. Second, you must give clear expectations. Help them make course corrections. Finally, make a change. Move on with them or without them.

The Bible declares, "Fear and intimidation is a trap that holds you back. But when you place your confidence in the Lord, you will be seated in the high place" (Proverbs 29:25 – TPT). Don't live in fear to the people you work with. It is a trap!

As a spouse. You will definitely not want to say, "Throw me off a cliff," after your next argument. It will not go well for you. In fact, they will probably throw you off that cliff. I would. Again, kidding. Proverbs 19:13 reveals that a "nagging wife can drive you crazy." I would also say a nagging husband can do the same! Notice, it says "can drive you crazy." It does not say "will." That means you choose how you respond to the craziness.

I wish I was more patient. It is definitely not a gift I was given. I am highly impatient. Still working on that one for sure! In the same way I will leverage tension in my workplace, I must also leverage it in my marriage! How do you leverage this tension? It's the big old "F" word: forgiveness. I must learn to forgive. I say this at nearly every wedding I officiate: "Marriage isn't the union of two great lovers as much as it is the union of two great forgivers." Forgive often and repeatedly!

As a parent. This is tough. I have three amazing kids. 99% of the time they are incredible. The other 1% they find ways to push me down a hill. But as a parent, I have to understand they are still growing and maturing before my eyes. That means I must lead my family with 'patience in the process." Yes, this is a struggle for me, but I am constantly trying to master this principle. Our kids need to see us model Jesus to them.

Isn't it amazing how one moment your child can have you laughing hysterically and then in a split second yelling? Tension. Yes, I have a teenager in my house (more to come) but I have to model the idea of love, care, and patience. Why? Because what Mary and I model, our kids will reproduce. We have to get it right!

As a child. As I have matured a little, I have found that my conversations with my mom have changed. She often pushes me to my limits, tests my belief systems, and adds stress to my day. But after all these years, I have never yelled at my mom, never hung up the phone on her, and never failed to say I love you – even after difficult conversations. Sometimes it feels like I am walking on broken glass - I am sure she feels the same. No matter what, I must always show respect. Never underestimate the power of respect. It is a lost art in the world, but one we need to find again.

As a friend. I truly want to be a better friend. It's an area I really try to work on, but there are some friends who are way worse than me. You know, the ones that don't return calls or text messages. They seldom ask, "How are you doing?" Yes, I have those friends too! We all do. I remember telling a pastor friend of mine about some physical challenges I was going through – I was pouring out my heart! – and in the middle he said, "Todd, sorry I have to run." He never once asked me how I was doing after that! I want to text him right now and say, "Push me down a hill," but I will not.

GRACE IS, 'I WILL STILL LOVE YOU EVEN WHEN YOU DO RUN OVER ME!

Grace. It's a word I grew up on and heard it all the time. The challenge is that everyone wants grace, but few give it. Grace is not, "Run over me." Grace is, "I will still love you even when you do run over me."

People will often try and project their personal saga into your life story. Protect yourself. Put up a wall but make sure it still has a door. My brother Kevin used to have a sign in one of his first homes that said,

"All of our guests bring happiness. Some by coming and others by leaving." Be the person that brings joy when you show up!

EVERYTHING SUCKS

Some of the toughest people to be around are those where everything sucks. It's true. The weather could be sunny, but they see it's too cold. The vacation was fantastic, but they remember how expensive it was. 1000 people showed up for church, but they complain about the lighting in the room. I am not sure why people are the way they are, but we are called to lead even difficult people.

So how do you lead people who live in the world called negative? *First, understand negativity comes from somewhere.* It did not just show up in that person's life. Try and understand why someone is the way they are. Put yourself in their shoes. So many people today are carrying around the baggage of their pain. They have never been healed of the abuse, loss, pain, or betrayal. They see everything from their negative lens because of what they have gone through. Strong leaders have an intuition that allows them to be able to see through the façade that people parade!

Second, don't take it personally. This is tough. To be honest, this is something I constantly battle! If we as leaders don't take it personally, our responses would be much different. Step out of what they are saying. The reality is negative people don't want to hear what you have to say, especially if it's the truth. They are so stuck in their past that they cannot enjoy today. Don't let their negativity sink into your heart.

Third, look for opportunities to speak openly! Have a conversation about the way they are speaking or behaving. Don't force it. It will happen at the right time. If you are an employer, it may come at the annual or semi-annual review. If you are a spouse, it may happen while watching television. If you are a pastor, you may see the open door after a stirring church service. Look for the opportunity. It will be there.

Finally, check your own heart. So often we read everything through the lens of our own experiences and then we mis-read people's responses or comments. As a leader, we must often check our own heart! Many times, it's an 'our' issue. Not every time, but many times. Try and see the good in everyone. Just because people go negative on you does not give you permission to go negative on them. Keep your heart right.

Mary and I were listening to a friend, Jeanne Munsey, speak with us over lunch and she said, "Hold loosely to what God has given you." Have you ever had a 'word' that came at the right time? This was one of those. We had a few people who lived like "everything sucks" and they attacked, criticized, and belittled us and our church. We really hate when people leave church, but in that moment, we chose to 'hold loosely' It was refreshing. It was liberating!

Leaders will always have emotional vampires around them. It does not matter how big someone gets or how successful they are, the vampires are out there. They will suck the very life out of your spirit. They will deplete your energy and discourage your dreams. Don't let them. It may mean limiting time with certain team members or even letting someone go. If you refuse to deal with the "everything sucks" person on your team, they will infect the rest of your team, which affects your business, church, or organization.

I GET SO EMOTIONAL

Every person ever created is unique. There are no identical people. Some people get more emotional than others. I am an emotional person. I cry watching Hallmark movies with my wife. That's really why I hate watching them! Leaders who get emotional have to learn very quickly to manage their emotions. Here's why: *If you can't manage your emotions, your emotions will manage you*! Every decision you make will be emotional. In the nearly 25 years I have been leading, I usually don't make good decisions when I am emotional, and neither will your team!

> **I CAN NEVER LET MY EMOTIONS TAKE CHARGE OF MY LIFE!**

Emotional people can take the air out of a room with their posture, blank stares, occasional loud gasps, and sarcastic tone. I had a staff member join our team; everything looked great. Then one day, while on a team trip, they exploded and then immediately became closed off! It was a 'wow' moment for every person on our team. Every single person was like, "I did not see that coming." It was out of the blue and unexpected. For the next 4 days, we all walked on eggshells. This created a lot of tension. Needless to say, that individual is no longer working for us.

You see, emotional people can be very good or they can be extremely bad. It all comes down to whether or not they have learned to manage their emotions. Inside each person is the tension between not being emotional enough and being too emotional, ultimately needing to learn how to leverage emotions.

As a communicator, I utilize the God-given gift of emotions. I like to take people on a journey! In one 35-minute talk, I want to see people laugh, cry, think, and get a little jittery. That's how you know you are touching the heart of someone. However, as a leader, I must make sure that my emotions are in check. I can never let my emotions take charge of my life. I must leverage my emotions and take charge of them!

Bishop T.D. Jakes said, "People who trespass on the emotional property of others' lives will someday find their own property invaded." How true is that? We must be very cautious how we deal with the emotions of other people, but also how we reveal the emotions in our own hearts!

Here are some examples of poor emotional management, which the Bible calls foolishness:

- *Saying whatever you think.* "I just speak my mind," while everyone else is thinking, "Leave some of it for yourself." The Bible says, "Only a **fool** speaks all that he knows (Proverbs 29:11)."
- *Being offended by correction.* Some people don't like to be told they are wrong – then they become offended by it. Proverbs 15:5 teaches that only a **fool** despises correction.

- *Not wanting to understand the other person*. This is a biggie. Most people want to be understood but they refuse to understand the other person's perspective. "A **fool** takes no pleasure in understanding" (Proverbs 18:2).
- *Quick to fight or argue*. There are a lot of hot-tempered people in the world today. They fly off the handle and say things they later regret. Proverbs 20:3 says, "Every **fool** is quick to quarrel."

Once again, if we can't manage our emotions, our emotions will manage us! As leaders, we have to leverage our emotions, but every emotion is not suitable for every environment! Leaders must develop a keen sense of discernment as to when and how to express themselves. Emotional leaders, like me, must work extra hard at this!

FOR THE HEALTH OF IT

Why is it important to have a strong emotional environment in your office, on your team, or in your church? That's the burning question. Here's the hot answer: *For the health of it*! If you want your organization to be healthy, it must have a level of emotional health. For me, if I want our church to be healthy, that means I have to guard and protect the emotional environment! One emotionally imbalanced staff member can destroy the chemistry on a team. That's why you must leverage the emotions in your workplace. For the health of it!

Now don't get me wrong, everyone has a bad day. That's not what we are talking about. We are talking about individuals, leaders, and team members who have a bad day, every day! There are way too many people like that. But for the health of your organization, you will have to make sure the morale of your business, church, or non-profit is not hijacked by unstable people!

Nothing can function properly in dysfunction! That's why every leader must pay the price in the beginning to protect the DNA. If the leaders won't protect it, then no one will. So, how do you create a functionally healthy organization? *First*, you will need to start in the hiring or recruiting process. Guard with everything you have who you bring onto your team. If they don't have the right attitude when they start, they probably won't have it when you let them go. Whether they are paid or volunteer, character trumps competency any day. For the health of it, bring on the right people.

Second, you will need to hold the line on expectations. Don't capitulate to people's views or opinions. Yes, they matter, but too many people try and change you or your organization with little change to themselves! I heard this principle years ago: *You will never get what you expect, but what you inspect.* Hold your team, organization, church, employees, or volunteers to higher expectations! For the health of it, keep your team accountability.

Third, examine what your team is reproducing. You teach what you know, but you reproduce who you are! If you have a team filled with lazy people, then your team leader is probably lazy. If you have a volunteer that always shows up late, then chances are their direct report is typically late too. Whatever you are, you will reproduce! Make sure you see what every person in your organization is reproducing. If you are not, then you will get what you have allowed. For the health of it, keep your team focused!

Finally, make changes quickly! Don't allow any personality to become a painful hangnail! Keep the environment healthy. One person who stays too long can destroy the immediate and long-term impact of your business or group. Would you ride a dead horse? No. Then don't ride a dead staff member either. For the health if it, let them go! For your sake and theirs!

MAKE SURE YOU SEE WHAT EVERY PERSON IN YOUR ORGANIZATION IS REPRODUCING!

Several years ago, one of the many pastors I had the privilege to work for and with, Paul J. Bartholomew said, *"Leaders can never lead with a glass jaw."* In other words, you have to take it on the chin from time to time. If a leader is emotionally unhealthy, it literally means they are leading with a glass jaw. When they get hit, their jaw (and their leadership) will shatter!

As a leader, you should never have to walk on eggshells with your team. If you are walking on eggshells with certain team members, then that means they might not be the right member for your team. Here's the good news: If you embrace the tension and not ignore it, you can rise above the individual conflict!

TENSION TIME

Look inside to see what changes can be made outside.

1. Which personality type drives you insane the most?

2. Do you have a negative personality, or do you just lead negative people? (Think about this question)

3. What team member do you walk on eggshells and broken glass around? Do you need to have an immediate conversation?

PART II

JESUS AND TENSION

If you follow the life of Jesus, you will quickly discover that His ministry had a lot of tension. "No way," you might think, "Jesus was a man of peace." Yes, He was (and still is), but tension was part of His life. Whether it was confronting religious leaders, healing on the Sabbath, eating dinner with tax-collectors and sinners, or telling one of His twelve disciples to betray Him quickly, you can see, tension was part of His life. Even Jesus' resurrection created tension!

How was Jesus able to leverage the tension that followed Him? The answer is simple: *He never allowed the tension inside.* You see, you can have difficulty surrounding you, but you can still have peace inside you. Too many leaders internalize instead of mobilize. If you simply hold everything inside, you will face countless health, emotional, and relational challenges. Jesus was able to center His life even though He faced tensions that you and I will never experience.

I am captivated by the calmness of Jesus as He is about to be arrested.

One of His own disciples is about to betray Him. Here is Jesus' response, "Judas, would you betray the Son of Man with a kiss?" (Luke 22:48 – NLT). The remaining disciples who are still with Jesus ask if they should fight; in the process, one of His disciples cuts off the right ear of one of the high priest's servants. Jesus says, "No more of this," picks up the ear, puts it in its place, and heals the man. Talk about a moment of tension.

Jesus used tension as an opportunity to teach. And yes, even heal. He made it part of the story. He knew how to leverage the tension around Him. Jesus had this incredible vision for the after-effect of every moment. His deity allowed Him to see beyond the current reality to the future possibility! He ultimately knew that the tension would not last forever. I think that's one of the biggest problems in leadership. We think tension is eternal. It is not!!!

Jesus knew that the present tension we experience is preparing us! I encourage our church all the time to never forget that God uses every pain and problem to prepare us for our potential! Tension is preparing us. You see, the tensions you survive today grow your capacity! Jesus understood that.

Fast-forward. Jesus is now on the cross. Talk about tension. I don't think any of us can connect with that, but that allows Jesus to connect with us (excuse the preacher moment). He is suspended on a wooden cross, hung between two thieves, and inching toward death. Jesus carries on conversations with multiple people: criminals, John, his mother, the soldiers, even God the Father. I am not sure I would have been able to muscle up the strength to say anything to anyone, but yet Jesus did.

I love this statement Jesus made – "Father, forgive them for they do not know what they are doing" (Luke 23:34 – NLT). In the middle of the greatest tension of His life on earth, Jesus leveraged it to speak to His Father on behalf of the people. Jesus knew that His tension would ultimately become our transformation.

TENSION HAS A PURPOSE

I truly believe that nothing is ever wasted. Not a moment. Not a day. Not a season. Everything that we experience or go through has a purpose. It's much bigger than you and I could ever imagine. Tension is a great teacher. It's the teacher no one wants, but everyone needs. Tension is not just good – it is vital. You cannot grow without tension.

TENSION IS NOT JUST GOOD – IT IS VITAL!

Do you remember feeling growing pains? You know, as a pre-teen, you had the aches in your knees and hips? All of us went through it. I know what I tell my kids: "That's normal." You see, every single person has growing pains. Some are more painful, but no matter who you are, if you are a human, you had growing pains. The same is true as a leader. You will have growing pains. Every conversation – good or bad – has a purpose in your life.

The Bible declares, "He always comes alongside us to comfort us in every suffering so that we can come alongside those who are in any painful trial. We can bring them this same comfort that God has poured out upon us" (2 Corinthians 1:4 – TPT). That verse teaches us that God gives us the ability to get through what life has brought us to so we can help others too! The tension you face today becomes someone's encouragement tomorrow. It has a purpose!

Several years ago, I battled a long season of anxiety. It was one of the most difficult struggles I had gone through personally. I faced a season of discouragement that was very dark and depressing. It took me 9 months to work through it and years to get back to normal. When I stood in front of my church and shared my struggle publicly for the first time, I never could have imagined the response. Dozens and dozens of people approached me sharing their struggle. I heard things like, "I thought I was the only one. I felt alone. I am glad someone finally shared their story." The truth is, we have so demonized mental health issues that people are unwilling to come out and share their struggle. I could not keep it in.

Now I am able to help others manage the tension of anxiety. I would have never been able to do that without going through it myself. Yes, there are still times I have to push the panic back, but I am so grateful that my tension has become a testimony to help others. Tension has a purpose.

The worst thing you can do is ignore the tension. You have to embrace it. Only when you embrace the tension, no matter what it is, will God reveal the purpose of it. I don't believe God causes it, but I do believe that He uses all things! Tension has a higher purpose for your life. It is used to develop you, not destroy you! Don't allow tension to bury you. God will use the tension that you are willing to leverage.

DON'T BE A KNEE JERK

There are people certain people in your life that knee jerk to everything they face. They overreact to emails, text messages, and conversations. Don't be that person. No one likes a knee jerk. But you also cannot ignore what you experience. There are many that try that, holding inside what they are experiencing or feeling. Totally unhealthy. The opposite is also unhealthy – to tell everyone how you feel about everyone and everything. Don't be a knee jerk.

A knee jerk jumps in without all the facts, sees things from only their perspective, and screams instead of converses! Yes, I have known a knee jerk … or 25. If I am being completely honest, I have been the knee jerk from time to time. Knee jerks come in all shapes and sizes, backgrounds and beliefs.

Jesus always seemed to respond appropriately to every situation He found Himself in. He spoke with patience to the woman caught in the act of adultery. He spoke with vision when He called the first 12 disciples. He spoke with conviction as He corrected the religious. He spoke with compassion as he approached the tomb of His friend Lazarus. Jesus found the right response to tense moments.

Now granted, aside from being fully man, He was fully God, so He had an advantage on many of us, but His life on earth teaches us the importance of responding to the tension we face with grace and conviction.

Several years ago, when we first started the church, it was very hard to get people to volunteer for our children's program. So, we made a decision to urge the parents who use the program to also serve in the program once a month. To Mary and I this seemed reasonable. But not everyone did, actually just one. This one person went all over social media and just bashed our church with statements like, "Volunteer means I don't have to. Watch out for charlatans who meet in movie theaters. Some churches don't know what the word volunteer means." There was also one post from this individual that compared me to the devil. Yep. I did not defend myself on Facebook. I simply picked up my phone and made a phone call. This was the only time I told someone to leave the church.

SILENCE DRIVES THE OPPOSITION INSANE!

Many times, leaders face tension and they openly respond. Here's what I have learned: *silence drives the opposition insane*. The online haters, the bold behind-your-back people, are looking for a social media fight. Refuse to cave in. Don't be a knee jerk.

Catch this: just because someone is a knee jerk, does not give you permission to be a knee jerk. No one likes jerks. But there is one group that people like even less – knee jerks.

A very wise friend, Bobby Petsiavas, gave me great advice several years ago. He said, "Always respond with the opposite spirit." Oh man, that is still good today. When someone has a critical spirit – bless them. When a person attacks you – stay silent. When the haters unleash social media insults – hold your peace. Just because your enemies do it does not give you permission to do it. Never stoop to the level of those beneath you! Let me write that again. Never stoop to the level of those beneath you! I needed to reread that as much as you did. In other words, don't let anyone control your reactions.

DISTRACTED

Jesus is enjoying dinner with His disciples. It is often called, "The Last Supper." They are all relaxing around the dinner table. Casually Jesus says, "I tell you the truth, one of you eating with me here will betray Me" (Mark 14:18 - NLT). Are you kidding me? I am so not Jesus. There is no way I would have been eating dinner with the person I knew was going to betray me. Jesus remained calm!

This was a very tense moment. How do we know? Because the disciples all began to argue with each other. I am sure that Judas remained silent or possibly pointed the finger at someone else. Jesus calmly told them the one who dipped his bread into the bowl with Him at the same time was the betrayer. It was none other than Judas. After he gets up and leaves, Jesus continues to talk to the disciples, leads them in communion, and then goes to Gethsemane to pray.

Jesus understood that tension was part of life. He did not let it overwhelm Him or get Him off mission. I think that is probably the greatest thing Jesus teaches us about tension – you cannot let it distract you!

I have faced many seasons of life and to be honest I have allowed many of those seasons affect me way too much. I have measured my success by my seasons – instead of by God's reasons! We have to learn to let God's "why" behind our "what" direct our lives. Don't get off mission. Stay focused on your calling. Jesus was a huge example of this.

One of the enemy's greatest tools against you is to distract you. If he can get you focused on your problems or your difficulties or on people, then he has the upper hand. Don't focus on those things. Use them as fuel but don't let them become a focus.

There are a few things that I do to stay focused. They are simple, but effective for me. *First, I remember what God told me in the first place.* If this sounds too simple, well… it is! Too often we get distracted because life gets too difficult, but you can't let those things determine your choices or you are ultimately out of control. Look back and remember what God spoke to you in the first place. I don't know if I should stay married – did God bring your together? I should never have started that business – did God direct you? I can't keep leading this church – did God call you? Look back.

YOUR FOCUS DETERMINES YOUR FORECAST!

Second, I know God has a proven track record. As I look back over my life, I can see how God's hand has been on me. He has opened doors for Mary and me that we could never imagine. As you examine your life, you will discover God has been looking out for you, opening and closing doors, directing your steps, and protecting your destiny!

You would not be where you are today without Him. He has used everything you have gone through to make you who you are!

Third, stay focused! This matters because your focus determines your forecast! If we constantly focus on everything wrong, all the reasons we can't, and what others say about us, we may never experience the life of excellence God wants for us.

A lack of focus makes room for the enemy. He comes in and tells you things about yourself that are not true: "You are not good" – "You won't get that job" – "You will never be healed" – "God does not have good plans for you" – "Your best days are behind you." You cannot allow these negative statements to take root in your spirit. Focus on what God has planned for you!

Jesus stayed focused. No matter what He went through or experienced, He knew why He was here. Don't get distracted. Stay focused! Don't let anything or anyone derail your destiny! Keep your eyes on the call God has put in your heart and the destiny He has placed over your life!

PUT YOUR FINGER HERE

Jesus had been crucified. Now, He had risen from the dead. He appeared to His disciples, but there was one who was not there – Thomas. When the other disciples told Thomas Jesus was alive, he basically said, "I have to see it to believe it." Eight days later Jesus appeared again. He walked straight up to Thomas and said, "Put your finger here, and look at my hands. Put your hand into the wound in my side. Don't be faithless any longer. Believe" (John 20:27 – NLT). Jesus did not get frustrated by Thomas' doubts. Instead, He addressed them.

There are a lot of leaders who get frustrated by the doubts of those we lead. Can you imagine this moment? Thomas must have felt like, "Oh man, it's really Him. I hope He doesn't call me out." But then Jesus did something so powerful. He did not call Thomas out, but He called him up. Big difference. He took Thomas from a place of doubt to fresh belief. He leveraged the tension of the moment!

How you respond to the doubts of those you lead is critical to your success as a leader. Jesus directly answered the doubts of Thomas with the facts. Thomas' response, "My Lord and My God." Thomas' doubts were eradicated by one moment with his leader. Jesus never ignored the questions of the leaders around Him. He may not have answered the way they would like, but He always had a response.

Where do you need to have someone put their finger? Is there a place in your leadership where people are doubting you or questioning your leadership? I am sure that has caused some tension. Remember tension is not a bad thing when you learn to leverage it. Let me give you some simple advice. *First, share the facts more than your feelings.* Too often leaders lead by emotions and that can become a very dangerous trend. The reality is our feelings change – but facts are facts. You cannot argue against those realities. For example, if you have an insubordinate employee who questions everything, share the facts of how that is affecting the team chemistry. This is huge – you are not responsible for how people respond to that conversation. You are simply responsible for how you share the facts.

Again, *those who are unwilling to grow with you cannot go with you.* Yep, this is the tough one to embrace, but just because you like someone as a person does not mean they are the right fit for you long term as a volunteer or even an employee. Every leader wants to see growth in people. For me, I find myself to be very slow in releasing someone from their job – but when I make the decision, it is immediate. I am patient because I hope for growth, long for it, and want to see it. But not everyone is designed to be with you long term.

The way I look at it, Jesus had twelve people really close to Him. Yet, one betrayed him, another denied knowing Him, and one more doubted Him. The rest scattered for a moment when Jesus was arrested. If that happened to Jesus, then it can happen to us!

In my humble opinion, Jesus was the best leader the world has ever seen, and He still faced tension on every level. But somehow Jesus found a way to leverage the tension of life and use it for a greater good!

Put your finger on the pulse of your leadership and ask yourself, "Where am I mismanaging the tension?" The answer to this question will help you better leverage your tension. We all mishandle the challenges we face – no one is perfect. But the key to leading like Jesus is learning from Him. Examine His life and ministry and you will continue to discover how well He leveraged the tension!

TENSION TIME

Look inside to see what changes can be made outside.

1. Jesus never allowed the tension inside. What tensions have you allowed to build a bitter root in your heart?

2. What attacks have you taken personally? How did you respond?

3. How do you respond to the doubts and critiques of those around you, especially those you lead?

RESIST AVERAGE

I love the story of Ruth in the Bible. Quick Sunday School lesson: Ruth is now living with her mother-in-law after the death of her first husband. Her mother-in-law encourages her to leave – to go back to her people. But Ruth stays faithful to her mother-in-law. She is now working in a field. She was a hard-working woman and she catches the eye of Boaz.

Not enough time to capture the whole story, but I love what her future husband says about her: "I will do for you whatever you ask, for all my people in the city know that you are a woman of excellence" (Ruth 3:11 – NASB). Ruth excelled. She worked hard and those around her noticed. She rose above the rest of the ladies. She went from working in the field to owning the field. She refused average.

I am confident "enough to get by" will never take you where you want to be. I believe that if you manage the smaller opportunities well, larger, better doors will open up for you. I have discovered: "You may never be the best – but you are always able to give your best." Jesus said, "If you are faithful in little things, you will be faithful in greater things" (Luke 16:10). Break the back of average by being excellent! The average person avoids pressure. The excellent person leverages it.

ENOUGH TO GET BY WILL NEVER TAKE YOU WHERE YOU WANT TO BE!

I am slightly OCD. It's true. Not in everything, but in many things. At home I am pretty relaxed. Mary manages our home life, so she keeps me focused. But at church I want everything done with excellence. I never want Church Unleashed to be the 'average' church. I want us to go above and beyond in every possible way. I am so bad at times that I even want every chair perfectly lined up. Here's why this matters so much: if I am preaching and the chairs are not lined up, it will bother me the whole sermon! A little crazy, right? Seriously, if someone can't do the small with excellence, they will never do the larger with excellence.

Every leader has their crazy. For me it is chairs, clearly. For the business person, it could be having their team arrive early to start the day. For the homeschool parent, it might be keeping to a tight schedule. For the college students, it is achieving the right degree from the right university to get the right job. If you are not excelling, it could be that you are not going above and beyond. Give your best in every moment and those moments will give their best back to you.

MINDSET MATTERS

Excellence starts in the mind. You see, if we flood our mind with negativity, we will become a product of our own thoughts. Like I stated before: *Your focus determines your forecast.* If we constantly focus on everything wrong, all the reasons we can't, and always see the glass as half empty, we may never experience the life of excellence we were designed for!

There is a great verse in the Bible about mindset. It says, "Stay alert! Watch out for your great enemy, the devil. He prowls around like a roaring lion, looking for someone to devour" (1 Peter 5:8 – NLT). In another translation of the Bible, it is worded as, "Be alert and of sober mind." To be sober means to keep your thoughts right – because if you don't have the right thoughts, the enemy is waiting for that negativity so he can devour you.

Negative thoughts give room for self-doubt. We have to keep a sober mind – looking at what is right and not letting negativity control our thoughts. People hear "**no**" or are told **what they can't do** *more than 148,000 times by the time they reach age 18*. What is the result? We program each generation to be negative before they go to college! Let's start reprogramming our thinking. Don't let the 1 negative comment someone said to you override the 7000 positive promises God has for you in the Bible.

Refuse to have a negative mindset. This is harder than it seems. I personally struggle with negative thoughts; I think we all do. Each day I have to fight the urge to go negative. I am so fixed on getting better that I often examine too much! "Fix this." "Change that." You can very easily allow a spirit of excellence, as a leader, to become a critical spirit! When that happens you see everything through the lens of negativity!

Every leader fights with this, especially the ones who are bent on getting better and better. So how do you protect your thoughts? *First, be very careful what voices you allow into your head!* Not every person should have access to your ear, nor should the majority have access to your heart. Have you ever been in a meeting where someone emotional hi-jacked it? I have. There are some people who have the gift of negativity. If you know them, run! Seriously, as a leader, you do not need "yes" people, but you need "yes, we can" people around you!

I struggle with my thought life. I think every leader does, whether they admit it or not. I feel at times like I will never be good enough and I am never as good as others. It is truly an issue that anyone with a pulse deals with – their thoughts! Because I struggle with the internal voices, I have to be more purposeful against the external voices.

WHAT YOU DON'T CONTROL WILL ULTIMATELY CONTROL YOU!

Second, learn to control your own inner dialogue. I have heard people say, "I can't control my thoughts." Bologna!!! I believe you can! Resist the urge to go negative on yourself. When a negative thought comes in, let it go right out! Talk yourself up. Remind yourself of every talent and gift that you possess. Don't meditate on your shortcomings and challenges! Control that dialogue. Evict those thoughts when they come in. Don't let them take root in the soil of your mind.

Never forget: what you don't control will ultimately control you. Your thoughts can take your life hostage. Guard those thoughts. A person who refuses to protect their mind will become one paranoid leader. Our mindset matters!

Finally, don't give life to your negative thoughts. Just because something comes into your mind does not mean it should pass through your mouth. Don't speak it. Don't share it. Don't post it. Let it pass through your mind, filter it, and then evict it.

Do you ever replay negative thoughts? I do. But just like my DVR at home, I have to delete to make room for more. If you want to be the leader God has called you to be, delete the negative thoughts and replace them with what your Creator says about you. You are good enough. You have what it takes. You are gifted, called, anointed, and appointed to achieve your destiny!

DON'T PLAY THE COMPARISON GAME

I am not a huge board game fan, but occasionally my two girls – Abigayl & Bethany – can get me to play. I am not sure why I don't – maybe because I grew up addicted to Nintendo playing all-night Tecmo Bowl and Pro Wrestling Tournaments (yes, I still love the 80s). But there is one game we should never play – The Comparison Game.

"If I had what they had, I would ..."

"If I was married to who they married, I could ..."

"If I had the money they had, I'd ..."

"If I had the staff they had, I could ..."

The comparison game will destroy your uniqueness. God likes the way He made you! You are one of a kind. You are special. You have a purpose. 2 Corinthians 10:12 teaches us not compare ourselves with anyone else. In other words, you will never be who someone else is because you are not them. Be you. In fact, be the best you that there could ever be.

Once you start comparing, the next thing that happens is complaining. "I hate my job." "I don't like this decision." "I can't believe they chose them." *When you compare, you despair*! It's a downward spiral. Don't fall into that trap. You are you. No one else will lead like you or live like you do!

There is a story in the Bible about King David, before he was king. He goes out to deliver some food to his brothers who were on the battlefield. David is young, ambitious, and confident. He can't believe Saul's greatest warriors will not fight Goliath. He says, "I will fight him." Saul says, "There's no way you can fight this Philistine and possibly win! You're only a boy, and he's been a man of war since his youth" (1 Samuel 17:23 – NLT). Saul just made the mistake of comparison.

David never compared himself to Goliath – he just trusted in God. Could you imagine if David let the words of Saul get in his head? David now sees Goliath and he starts to think, "Look at the size of Goliath. I am just a boy." He could have run in the opposite direction, but David knew better and declared, "You come to me with sword, spear, and javelin, but I come to you in the name of the LORD" (1 Samuel 17:45 - NLT). In other words, "I am not you, but I have a secret weapon – His name is God." You do not need to be anyone but you. Be the best you that you can be. Don't compare.

The Bible declares, "Pay careful attention to your *own work*, for then you will get the satisfaction of a job well done, and *you won't need to compare yourself to anyone else*" (Galatians 6:4 – NLT, *emphasis mine*). Focus on your own life. Don't get tied up comparing yourself to anyone. You are a one-of-a-kind creation. Hand made by God to be an incredible leader in this world.

When Mary and I first started our church, I had no idea what kind of pastor I would be. I was so insecure. I tried a few styles trying to figure this thing out. I taught from a stool, I dressed up, and tried to mirror some successful pastors. Only one problem - I was not them! Ultimately, I decided to just be me! I can't compare myself to anyone else.

It's too exhausting competing and comparing. I would rather just be the best version of me that I can be. Don't try and be a carbon copy of someone else. Be you. There is only one you that was ever created. Focus on you. If you attempt to be someone else, you will be miserable. It's impossible to be someone else because you are not someone else.

LIVE CONTENT

I grew up in a lower middle-class income family. My mother worked very hard to provide for her three sons. You know you are in need when you are eating government issued peanut butter in the white can with black letters that said, "PEANUT BUTTER" (side note, I learned later in life that I am allergic to peanut butter. Thank God for His protection).

Back to contentment. At an early age, I learned the principle of being content with the basics, just enough. Hey, as long as I had food, shelter and clothes, I was doing pretty good! You don't have to have the best to be blessed, if you are just content!

Now as adults, Mary and I try to be content with what we have. It is not always easy. Yes, there are times I have the urge to crave a Lexus or a Beemer or an Audi, but the cars we currently have are just fine. We are blessed because we choose to be content! Contentment is a state of spirit, not mind. You see, if it's a *state a mind,* I will never be content because my mind always compares, but if it's a *state of spirit,* my soul will self-correct! Yes, mindset matters, but spirit matters more!

As a leader, there is a unique balance between contentment and progress. Every leader wants to go forward. However, few leaders choose to grow forward! Leadership is about being content where you are, but at the same time pushing forward. It's not an easy thing to balance. That's why not everyone is a leader!

In the midst of your progress, take time to enjoy how far you have come and where you currently are. Most leaders never do. They go from project to project, employee to employee, success to success, failure to failure, and year to year never hitting the pause button. Buy yourself a steak, go on a vacation, or purchase a new outfit to celebrate your journey.

I have come a long way since government issued peanut butter, but I am so grateful for my start in life. It taught me to be okay with what you have. I don't need more to be happy. I just need to be okay with what I have.

CONTENTMENT DOES NOT MEAN SETTLE!

Let me say this though: *contentment isn't a synonym for laziness*. Oh yes, I did. I talk to leaders all the time who are not content – they are lazy. I have heard them say, "I am happy where our company is – I can just show up." What?! Are you kidding me? Remember, contentment is a *state of spirit* because our mind will never be content. Contentment does not mean "settle for average." No, it simply means you will always be grateful for every step of the journey you experience, good or bad. Live content.

EMBRACE THE RAT RACE

Working 9 to 5 is more like 9 to 9 today. It has become more and more difficult to disconnect. People are working, commuting, and communicating around work more than ever before. It's part of the process of life. If you are going to rock contentment, you will have to embrace the rat race of today. It gets hectic. Schedules get jammed. Things are overlooked. Stop, smile, and embrace it, keeping these thoughts in mind:

You will never be perfect. This is a difficult one to embrace but every leader wants to be perfect. In reality, there are no perfect people! Take a risk. Try something new. Put yourself out there and solve a problem your boss does not know exists! If you fail – at least you will have tried. That's the nature of the leaders who break the back of average. They try even though they may not get it right or have all the answers!

You may get overlooked. Growing up in Gen X, I know this is a tough one for millennials to grasp. For decades we were taught, "Get out there, give your best, whether or not anyone notices." Today I find that young leaders want what they have not worked for. Catch this: You may never get the recognition you deserve but keep working. Someone will notice!

You will have to work harder than others on your team. There will always be slackers in every job (if they work for a great company, they won't last long). Don't lower yourself to their limited capacity. Keep growing. Work harder than others and you will get what others will not. Set yourself apart by excelling in the rare commodities of blood, sweat, and tears!

You will feel stressed out and overwhelmed. As a leader, I have more days where I feel overwhelmed than I would like to admit. They are there. They are real. Stress is a big tension. Embrace the reality that life will cause stress. Don't try and run from it. Admit your stress. Don't deny your feelings. Every leader faces stress. If they tell you they don't, they are lying. It's true. Learn to manage the stress. It can actually help you focus, reset, and push forward.

You will be late for dinner. Yes, Mary hates this one. But as God has allowed us to experience some level of success, it has created more work, which equals later hours. Some leaders never get in trouble with their spouses for being late for plays, dances, family events, or dinners. Not me. I find myself late because of the blessing of success. It has added more work, but it's rewarding work.

You will face criticism. If you can't handle the attacks, stay out of the battle. Over the nearly 25 years I have had the privilege to lead, I have had my fair share of criticism. Now I just expect it. If you don't want to be criticized, do not do anything! Sit home on your couch watching Netflix and eating chocolate. The life of a leader is a life that creates criticism.

Embrace the rat race. Stay content. Don't be lazy. Keep your mindset right and do not play the comparison game. Now, go out there and prove your critics wrong. Do something great!

TENSION TIME

Look inside to see what changes can be made outside.

1. Are there some smaller things that you have been mismanaging?

2. What causes you the least contentment? Why?

3. What have you been resisting that is just a part of life? How can you make an internal adjustment?

ART OF THE PIVOT

I love football. I played football from 3rd grade to 11th grade. It was a long and exciting career from Pop Warner to high school. To be honest, I wanted to be the next Jerry Rice. One major problem – there is only *one* Jerry Rice. As a wide receiver, I had to master something that many young football players do not. I had to learn how to pivot. Every route I ever ran as a receiver had hard pivots attached to them. Why? Because the stronger my "cuts" or pivots, the more likely I would find myself open for a reception.

Without the ability to pivot, there is no way to leverage the tension. Pivoting is all about being able to adjust to new circumstances. Too many people live life with no flexibility. Being able to adjust is one of the most important ingredients for leadership. Things change. If you are unwilling to pivot, you may miss out on incredible opportunities.

When Mary and I first started our church, God gave us a very clear strategy. We felt in our spirits that we were to launch multiple church campuses across Long Island. It seemed like a daunting task as we were just starting our church. Nevertheless, that's what we felt so we have embraced that mission. Imagine our surprise when 3 years into our journey, our denomination gifted us another building with a parsonage. It was simply given to us. We had already purchased our first building and now we were getting a gift building. We felt like someone needed to pinch us.

If God never gave us a vision for multiple locations, we would never have accepted the gift. The only condition was we had to establish a church there. No problem. We gave it a run. Hired a campus pastor, cleaned the building, emptied the garbage, and started holding services. It was a difficult 18 months. We could not break the forty-five-person barrier.

Let me tell you, we faced difficulty in that place. The building needed more repairs than we could afford, the village was being difficult, and the church was not growing. I had to make a change. So, I decided to shut it down. People were upset, but Mary and I knew in our hearts it was the right thing to do. We did it with no apology!

It was time for a pivot.

Way too long of a story to go deep into, but we ultimately sold the church and parsonage, purchased our 30,000 square foot main campus with the proceeds of the property and renovated the majority of the building. If we did not pivot, we would have been struggling for years. God used that property to propel us forward.

I had someone several years ago get frustrated with my decision-making when something was not working. They said, "You change too quick." Remember my advice in a previous chapter? My response was simple and probably a little sharp: "*How long do you ride a dead horse? You don't. You get off and find a new horse.*" No leader should waste days, months, or years of their lives continuing things that are failing. Sometimes you have to pivot!

DIG A NEW WELL

There is a story in the Bible where Isaac is planting his annual crops. That year he harvested 100 times more grain than he planted because "the Lord blessed him" (Genesis 26:12 – NLT). The Bible declares, "He became a *very rich man*, and *his wealth continued to grow.* He acquired so many flocks of sheep and goats, herds of cattle, and servants that *the Philistines became jealous of him*" (Genesis 26:13-14 – NLT, *emphasis mine*). So, the Philistines find his wells and fill them all up with dirt. Why does this matter? Water matters. No water means no crops. No water means no cattle. No water means no life, no profit, no future. Talk about tension!

> **NO LEADER SHOULD WASTE DAYS, MONTHS, OR YEARS OF THEIR LIVES!**

Have you ever been in a place where everything was going great and then all of a sudden, things changed: the attack came, the sickness settled in, the problems escalated? That's where Isaac was. His well had run dry. Isaac had to now find a new well – *he had to pivot.* So, he moved to Gerar to dig a well, where fresh water flowed. Their prayers were answered, but the shepherds of Gerar argued and claimed the well that Isaac's servants dug. "This is our water," they said. Isaac's men had to *pivot again* to dig another well. They found a new well, but then another dispute rolled out. *Another pivot*. The tension was intense!

I am sure you, like me, have had times when you were digging wells where you thought God sent you and all you did was face opposition and problems. Everywhere you turn, you face disappointment, difficulty and discouragement. We all face this from time to time. But then I love this next portion of Scripture: "Abandoning that one, Isaac moved on and dug another well ..." (Genesis 26:22 - NLT). Don't get stuck crying over the things that did not go your way - move on. Abandon the wells of failed relationships, sinful pasts, personal disappointments, deteriorated health, missed opportunities, or declining dreams. Pivot!

Isaac is now moving to a place called Beersheba. He arrives and God appears to him. Here's what God says, "Do not be afraid, for *I am with you* and *will bless you. I will multiply* your descendants, and they will become a great nation" (Genesis 26:24 – NLT, *emphasis mine*). Isaac hears a word, builds an altar, and worships God. Does he sit back and tweet about it? Post a selfie with his handmade altar? Do nothing? No! The Bible says, "He set up his camp at that place, and his servants *dug another well*" (Genesis 26:25 – NLT, *emphasis mine*). Isaac and his men had to master the art of the pivot or they would never had been able to leverage their tension.

Keep digging wells of your destiny. Don't let one failure, one difficulty, one problem keep you from blazing new trails and making a difference in this world.

"But I have been down for so long."

"I don't know if I have the strength."

"I am too broken."

Don't stay stuck! Refuse to let failed business decisions or personal problems keep you running the same route. Pivot! If you cannot pivot, you will never be able to leverage your tension. For the sake of your leadership, pivot!

GOD LEVERAGES TENSION

If you have ever faced an attack, you are most likely not thinking in the middle of it: "Ok, God what are you preparing me for?" No, we are usually thinking, "Get me out of this!" God allowed Isaac to experience some closed wells to finally land the "right one." Continuing in our story, he was digging this well in Rehoboth and listen to what he said, "**At last** the LORD has created enough space for us to prosper in this land" (Genesis 26:22 – NLT). In other words, *finally*! God used all the opposition and tension to reposition Isaac.

> **ALL OF US LIVE BETWEEN THE TENSION OF NOW AND NOT YET!**

The truth is, sometimes we are just way too stubborn, stuck in our ways, and resistant. God sometimes has to leverage some difficulty to reposition us, fix our attitudes, or re-align our spirit. It's the part of life that none of us enjoy, but all of us need. God has this incredible way of using everything we experience for a picture that He has created, but we have not seen. As leaders, we have to trust that God is leveraging the tension, stress, and difficulty to bring out the best in us!

Israel is leaving Egypt. They just spent 430 years in slavery. The Bible declares, "God did not lead them along the main road that runs through Philistine territory, even though that was the shortest route to the Promised land" (Exodus 13:17 – NLT). God sends them on a little detour. The Scripture goes on to say that "God led them on a roundabout way through the wilderness ..." (Exodus 13:18 – NLT). Talk about tension. There was a shorter route, but God sent them a different way!

Have you ever felt like you are on a "roundabout way" to your destiny? Did you ever think God was using a small detour to bring you to your big destiny? All of us live between the tension of now and not yet. It's true. We want everything now, but life says not yet. There are so many things I thought I would have accomplished by now, but they haven't happened yet. For some, "I should have been married by now." "I should have been the CEO by now." "I should have had kids by now." "I should have done something more by now."

Scripture declares, "And we know that God causes everything to work together for the good ..." (Romans 8:28 - NLT). That even includes the tension you are experiencing! Hold on to the promise that everything will work out at the right time. It may not be now, but it will happen.

Don't force a door open! God will leverage your tension with His timing and get you to where He designed you to be in life and leadership!

ROADBLOCKS TO PIVOTING

No matter how comfortable we get, we can't get so comfortable that we refuse to make the right pivots or adjustments. That requires honesty. You and I have to be honest about what changes we need to make – we have to pull the layers back and determine the changes that will help our situation.

No matter what happens in life, we can expect change! Most of us don't avoid change – but we avoid changing ourselves! How true is that? I think we should embrace change and tension – because they help us become a better version of ourselves! That's the art of the pivot! You cannot avoid change or tension – you must embrace it!

Why do we avoid change? Here are a few reasons:
- **Comfort** – we settle in to what we are familiar with.
- **Laziness** – we just don't want to change.
- **Fear** – we are afraid of the unchartered territory.
- **Content with the minimum** – we are good with just enough to get by.
- **Lack of trust in God** – we can't understand why God does or allows certain things.

You see, what you think affects how you act. That's why it is so hard to pivot. Unfortunately, change is impossible unless you recognize those things that are controlling you. You might be controlled by ambition, greed, or popularity, physical appearance, your desire for power, or what others think of you. Don't be controlled, be changed!

There is a story in the Bible about a man named Gideon. Gideon finds himself threshing wheat, separating the grain from the chaff. On the surface, no big deal. Problem was, Gideon was hiding at the bottom of the winepress so he could have money for his family because times were tough, and he was afraid. But an angel of the Lord appears to him and says, "MIGHTY WARRIOR!" Gideon basically responds, "Angel, I am here hiding, threshing wheat. I am not a mighty warrior." God was about to change Gideon's destiny. The angel pushes back: "The Lord is with you, mighty warrior" (Judges 6:12 – NLT).

In the end, God grew Gideon. His small army defeated the impossible Midianite enemy. His army started at 32,000 and dwindled down to 300 – but it was led by a mighty warrior who leveraged the tension of change!

We all have areas of our lives where we wonder why people left us or why this or that happened. But change is unavoidable. Things will always change! Don't fight it. Leverage change! It's a great tension teacher! Learn to pivot!

MAKE PRE-DECISIONS

A concept I've come to love, and embrace is that of making pre-decisions. It's pretty simple but I believe it can save people from a world of hurt! What is a pre-decision? It is a decision you make before you have to make that decision – kind of like changing before you have to.

Let me give you some examples:
- "Should I not have sex with this person?" is not the decision you make when you are in the back seat of your car making out!
- "Should I not leave work an hour early and not tell anyone?" is not something you determine when its 95 degrees outside and you have already left the building.
- "The cashier gave me too much change – should I go back and give it to her?" is not something you should decide after you have spent the extra money.

NO ONE ELSE IS RESPONSIBLE FOR YOUR DECISIONS BUT YOU!

Pre-decisions are about making decisions before you have to! Here's some good pre-decisions we should make:
- I will be faithful to prayer and Bible reading even when my schedule gets crazy.
- I will honor my future spouse by not having sex until marriage
- I will honor my marriage even when things are not perfect.
- I will love my kids even if they drive me nuts.
- I will tithe even when my funds are tight.
- I will help those around me even when I don't feel like it!
- I will be loyal at work.
- I will be the best friend I can to as many people as I can.
- I will be honest.

What pre-decisions do you need to make? Pre-decisions make the pivot so much easier! If you make the decisions before you have to make the decision, it makes the decision easier! Phew! That is a mouthful but when the pressure is turned up, keeping this sentiment in mind makes the decision-making process easier. Like I shared before, you should never make decisions based on pressure, but purpose. Purpose is determined before the pressure arrives.

No one can make pre-decisions for you. You have to make them by yourself. Yes, you can ask for outside input, but at the end of the day, they must be your decisions. Here's why: *no one else is responsible for your decisions but you*! Talk about tension. As a leader, the "buck stops with you," and you cannot blame anyone for your bad decisions. This is why pre-decisions are so important. The more pre-decisions you make, the less tension you will experience.

Pre-decisions are based on values, purpose, and goals. They help you gauge what it truly important in your life. Without them, the tension will overwhelm us. With them, we are able to leverage the tension we face.

Make the pre-decision to start making pre-decisions. It will save your life from a lot of hurt and your leadership from lots of wasted time. Pre-decisions are gifts. They create boundaries, protect your schedule, and secure your integrity!

DON'T HESITATE

Have you ever heard the expression, "He who hesitates is lost?" I am sure you have. Hesitation has its roots in insecurity. We live unsure. We lead unsure. We don't pivot because we are insecure about the decision we are about to make. Every decision we make should be clear and precise!

The Bible reveals that, "thousands upon thousands are waiting in the valley of decision" (Joel 3:14 – NLT). In other words, there are crowds of people stuck in the valley because they cannot make a decision. Don't be one of them. Refuse to follow the crowds to the valley. Ascend to your destiny! Climb higher. Don't stay in the valley just because everyone else is in the valley!

Too many people and leaders push the pause button on life! They stay stuck in the valley for the rest of their lives. But here's the thing: *The pause button was not designed to be permanent*!

Make a decision. If you must, pivot!

TENSION TIME

Look inside to see what changes can be made outside.

1. Where do you need to make pivots in your life or leadership?

2. What pre-decision do you need to make so you don't have to make a pressured decision?

3. You need to be able to pause from time to time, but where have you hit the pause button where you should be making adjustments?

LET THEM WALK

One of the hardest things to learn in life is letting go of the wrong people. I am going to dedicate a whole chapter to this because most people walk with the wrong people so long that they end up in the wrong destiny. You see, I had to learn early in life that if people can't embrace your destiny, you have to make them part of your history. Not every person you meet will be your greatest fan or cheerleader. Too often we try and live to make people happy so much that we forget to make ourselves happy.

If someone can't support your dreams, let them walk. If they can't cheer for you, or stand beside you, or support you, let them walk. You do not have to take everyone into your future. Here is what I know: *everyone may want to go with you, but not everyone will want to grow with you.* What does that mean? I am so glad you asked. Some people like you "small" because that keeps them bigger than you.

Several years ago, I had a family try to control everything I did. They attempted to use manipulation to force my hand. It was a very difficult time. At one point I had enough. Yes, it hit the fan, but honestly, I felt an immediate freedom. The wrong people will try to hijack who you are and what you are designed to do. Some people want you to stay small because then they will seem more important. But as you grow, not everyone will be able to go with you.

SOME PEOPLE WANT YOU TO STAY SMALL BECAUSE THEY WILL SEEM MORE IMPORTANT!

If people can't handle your success or your leadership or your convictions, let them walk. *Don't bring people into your destiny who belong in your history*! Leaders who accomplish much have an intuition for who to walk away from. Think about it right now: Who in your life should you not bring into your future? It sounds like a harsh question, but in reality, you are helping both people! Sometimes people are too stubborn to walk away from a non-positive friendship or relationship and they need help. Make a choice. Be decisive.

If someone is holding you back and you do nothing, you are to blame. Get some courage! It's not going to be easy to change your relational circles, but in order to rise higher, you can't have the weight of negative relationships holding you back. Shake off those people who seem to keep you under their thumb of control or a critical attitude. You have to be so focused on your future that you let people walk who don't belong there!

Guard who you allow near you.

Protect your space!

THE RIGHT CIRCLE

I have discovered that some of the greatest challenges in our spiritual life are often caused by who we allow into our spiritual life! Who we allow to speak into our decisions, beliefs, and direction is part of our spiritual growth. If we are going to become all that God has designed for our lives, we have to choose the right circles of influence! The Bible teaches that "bad company corrupts good character" (1 Corinthians 15:33 – NLT). In other words, you will become who you surround yourself with!

If you are around negative people, you will become negative. If you choose friends who gossip, you will evolve into a gossip. But the opposite is also true. If you surround yourself with "Yes, you can" people, you will go after the dream God has placed in your heart! If you put godly people in your "circle," you will become more and more like Jesus. Scripture says it this way: "*Don't befriend* angry people or associate with hot-tempered people, or *you will learn to be like them and endanger your soul*" (Proverbs 22:24-25 – NLT, *emphasis mine*). You see, the people or influences we allow into our relational circles can do something so damaging – they can endanger our spirituality!

Let me ask you today, who is influencing you? Are you hanging with the right people? Or are you settling for the wrong people? Friend, your circle will determine your choices! You want to stay discouraged? Circle yourself with discouraged people! You want to live with hope? Put faith-filled people in your circle. Your circle will determine your choices – they will affect every decision you make. That's why you have to choose the right circles!

Jesus had His circles of relationship. The first circle Jesus had was the **RELIGIOUS**. Jesus was not close to this group. He kept them at a distance. The religious were the critical, negative voices in the backdrop of Jesus' story who felt they truly lived godly lives. Jesus spent little to no time with the wrong people!

The next circle Jesus had was the **CROWDS**. These were those that followed Jesus, listened to His message or were looking for His miracles. There were tens of thousands. This group wanted something from Jesus. The crowds demanded Jesus time and attention.

Then you had the **FOLLOWERS**. They were the committed core. There were individuals like Lazarus, Mary, and Martha. They were not looking for what they could get out of Jesus. They just wanted simple friendship. But there were so many. This group is not going to bring you down, but their objective is not necessarily to always refresh you. They will cheer you on from the sidelines. We all need those people.

Then Jesus had His **DISCIPLES**, twelve men who He brought very close. Dinners. Missions. Object lessons. Empowerment. Teaching. He spent a lot of time investing in them because He knew their potential. There are people God places in our lives to DEVELOP - to help them GROW to the next level.

But Jesus had one more group, **THE INNER CIRCLE**. Peter, James, and John. Just three people. These were the 3 that Jesus spent the most time with and made the greatest investment in. Three out of thousands and thousands of people. These are our BFF's - the one's we are closest to - the ones you can trust. Notice, Jesus closest circle was VERY small.

He did not allow everyone in His circle. After all, your friends will help determine your future!

Your circle determines your cycle. Guard who you allow in. Be careful. Let me say that again: Be careful. That does not sound even hard enough! **Be extremely careful** who you allow in! Let me say that again. Be extremely careful who you allow in! Whoever has your ear directs your heart! Don't let just anyone into your space. Create and maintain boundaries!

LET GO

If you don't let go of the wrong people, you will never experience the right people. This is difficult, but we have to choose our friends very wisely. You may need to change some of the friends you are hanging with. "But Todd, I won't have any friends." Don't worry about that! God will send you the right friends, better friends. If you are filling your time with the wrong, you will never have room for the right. Proverbs 14:7 reads, "Stay away from fools, for you won't find knowledge on their lips (NLT)." The Bible is telling us that we should not circle up with those who continually make unwise decisions. Why? Because God knew that we would become like who we spend the most time with. If we are spending time with the wrong people, we will never become the right people!

Guard who you allow in your circle! Let go of the friends or relationships that are dragging you down. God will bring the right people into your life at the right time - all you have to do is make some room. God is not going to force you to change your influences, but if you want to experience real joy, you have to make room for the right people. The wrong people will keep you from the right destiny.

People are like elevators; they will take you up or down. The wrong people will block, stop, and discourage your destiny. Scripture declares, "Walk with the wise and become wise; associate with fools and get in trouble" (Proverbs 13:20 – NLT). You see, if you want to discover your destiny, you have to surround yourself with LIFE-GIVING people! You can't grow around dead people. Some of us have been stuck in our situations simply because we are hanging with everyone else who is stuck. They are not encouraging us to rise higher because they have settled. Others are spending time with friends that are negative influences.

PEOPLE ARE LIKE ELEVATORS; THEY WILL TAKE YOU UP OR DOWN!

Did you ever have any friends that "caused" you to get in trouble? You know, maybe when you were a teenager? You knew you should not do that one thing, but they kept egging you on! What did you do? You did it! The wrong people will keep us from the right things. That's why we need to surround ourselves with the right people.

Not every person who starts with you is designed to stay with you. It seems like a very cold statement, but not everyone around you is your fan. Behind the scenes, there are people in your life that are tearing you down, lying about you, and hoping you fail. I have had my share. As a leader, you have to learn to let go of people. If you do not, those individuals remain in control of your life and leadership. They ultimately derail your destiny.

Remember, you do not need "Yes People" in your life either. You do need "Yes, We Can People!" It is important that you put the right people in your corner if you are going to become all God made you to be, but that often means getting the wrong people out of your corner first!

Over the years of hiring and firing people, I have had my share of challenging people. Most of the people that I released from employment were pretty good, but then there are those who confirm your decision as a leader by how they act after you let them go. I have learned that if someone gets divisive *after they left,* they were causing division *before they left!* It always comes to the surface. The only thing I often regret in dealing with people like this is that I did not act sooner! Be decisive. Act quick. Let go of the wrong people.

CHOOSE WISELY

One of the most difficult challenges a leader must overcome is who they choose to be a part of their team or circle of friends. The relational choices you make will automatically generate something. Choose wisely. Our Executive Pastor, Gina Bellomo, made a statement in a staff meeting: "You can make your own choices, but you do not get to choose your consequences." How true is that? That's why you have to make wiser choices on the front end. You will save yourself a lot of headache and heartbreak if you make smarter choices – not just relational, but in every area.

So, how do you make a great choice? I am not talking about just a good choice, but a great choice! Every leader has to learn to make better hiring decisions, in business and in life. *First, choose character over competency.* I truly want someone in my corner that has integrity. Skills can be learned, but character is pre-defined by internal beliefs. I heard this before, which is a great reminder for me: "Don't believe someone's press release." People can make themselves look really good on paper and that's it! Surround yourself with people that are honest even when it is difficult. Find the people you would want to be like and bring them into your circle.

Second, choose beyond gender. As a pastor, I have made a simple choice – I would rather have the right person than the right gender! If the best choice for the position is a male, I will hire him. If the best choice is a female, I will hire her. It's pretty simple to me, yet our world still seems at times to have a male-driven agenda. To me, it is simply about who is best equipped to do the task at hand. Focus on the greatness someone has on the inside!

Third, choose those who compliment you. What do I mean by that? Surround yourself with people who are not like you. They have different skills, but also see things from a different perspective. My wife, Mary, is like that. She sees things that I cannot see. Why? Because she is different than me. God brought her into my life as a compliment to what I needed. Mary sees my blind spots, but she also will see other people's intentions before I do. She has incredible discernment!

Someone once said, "Staff your weakness." I like that. Put people that are brighter, smarter, and better than you on your team! If you do not leverage the tension of people placement, you will never have the right people in the right place.

Finally, choose teachable team members. Know-it-alls drive me insane. Talk about tension. I can't stand it when I am speaking with someone about a topic I know to be true, and they will argue with me just because. I can feel my blood pressure going up right now. Ugh. Argh. Ok, breath. There are people in this life that will always think they know everything. Surround yourself with people that want to learn, grow, and become.

THEY WERE NEVER WITH YOU

In 2018, we faced one of the toughest years of our ministry. Over the previous nine years since launching our church, we had seen growth in every area. It was not always easy, but we had to simply keep leveraging the tensions we would face. But 2018 was a tough year. We had many people move out of state – the most we had ever experienced. We experienced betrayal from unexpected people. We watched social media smear campaigns try and discredit our character. Through it all, Mary and I remained silent and steadfast. We chose not to respond to the negativity, lies, and attacks. They were very hurtful. Some cut deep, but I had to consider the source.

> **WATCH OUT FOR THOSE WHO ALWAYS TELL YOU THAT THEY NEVER SPEAK TO ANYONE!**

Here's what I learned over those twelve months: *just because someone says they are for you does not mean they are for you.* You see, in front of us they were cheering us on, but behind our backs they were making subtle and not-so-subtle comments. We were committed to simply moving forward. Side note: Watch out for those who always tell you they never speak to anyone else. Over nearly 25 years of ministry I can honestly tell you they are usually the ones talking to everyone!

You see, if they can attack you, criticize you, and stab you in the back, they were never in your corner. You did not lose them – they simply revealed who they were! They were never with you. They worked with you, lived with you, or worshipped with you for what they could get out of you. When they drained you, they were done with you! Here's my simple advice: *let them walk.*

The tension may be intense for a season, but in the long run you will see God's hand of destiny revealed in your life. When things rise to the surface and you deal with those issues, it will never be easy. But after the dust settles and the smoke clears, you will have a peace that you did not have before. *Let them walk.*

When I reflect on my life, here is what is so amazing. Despite the difficulty, we are stronger than ever before. Our team chemistry, vision, finances, and overall health of the church has drastically improved overnight! You see, when someone is not for you, their words spread, and they cause an infection. Whether in church, business, home or friendship circles, the wrong person(s) can poison the culture you are trying to create. It may be hard to let them walk, but I promise the short-term tension will be worth it! If you are like me, desiring to protect your culture, then make sure you don't let those who are not with you, stay with you. *Let them walk.*

I have learned if you don't walk away from the relationships that hold you back, you won't have room for the life-giving relationships that God has designed for you! Don't hold on to the people who are weighing you down! "How do I know who that is?" Great question! Start with asking yourself, "Who do I avoid on my team?" Tough question, but a question you have to ask. Or how about this, "Who does everyone have a problem with?" If your team is coming to you about so-and-so, then leverage the tension and have the tough conversation. In the end, you may have to *let them walk.*

If you cannot let the people go who are crippling your creativity, or stifling your specialty, or manipulating your movements, then you will remain stuck in your current tension. Leverage it. Work through it. Tough it out. Suck it up. *Let them walk.*

TENSION TIME

Look inside to see what changes can be made outside.

1. How many friendships do you need to have to make you feel important?

2. Which people closest to you should not be as close as they are?

3. Are you the friend, family-member, staff member, employer that others want to be or the one others want to avoid? What changes do you need to make?

PART III

A GIFT CALLED GRACE

In 2013, God put it on my heart to send a letter to my father – the man who abandoned my mom and brothers when I was about 2 years old. Despite having no relationship with him for over 40 years, I felt compelled to send a letter. The problem was that every time I wrote it, I felt like I could not get the correct words! It was a tense season. My amazing wife, Mary, kept encouraging me.

On June 11, 2013, I finally sent the letter. Let me share a small portion of that letter with you.

"Dear Ronald:

I have tried to write this letter dozens of times, but never seemed to find the right words to express my thanks to you for bringing me into this world. I was just thinking about Father's Day and thought I would finally have the courage to send you a note.

Although your marriage with my mother did not last – you were instrumental, to say the least, in bringing life to three boys (Kevin, Scott & myself) – and for that I will always be thankful for you. Without you, I would not exist today!

Growing up was not easy for me. But the challenges that I faced growing up made me who I am today. I have become a driven, hard-working and motivated leader. I believe that my past prepared me for what I am doing today! I would love to have been part of a "normal" family, but God had a different plan/journey for my life. There were times I would have loved to hear my father say, "Son, I am proud of you," but I never did – but I know my Heavenly Father was and is. We did not have the best of things growing up, but that taught me to be thankful for every little thing that I own or experience ..."

Skipping ahead …

I am not writing because I want or need anything. I simply want you to know that I hold nothing against you or my upbringing. I am not angry, bitter or hateful about my life. I am so grateful to God for the life I have. I treasure every single day. There are no expectations I have other than letting you know I am forever grateful for the gift of life that you gave me ..."

4 days later I received a response. It was a Father's Day card. Let me share his response.

"Todd. I am glad you are happy and doing well. I am sorry for missing so much of your life, you have always been in my heart ... hearing from you was a great Father's Day gift. I am so proud of you and the man and father you have become. Love, Dad."

You see, although I had already forgiven my father many years ago, I never let him know! That was not grace. Grace shares what God has done in you and through you! Here's what I have learned by walking through this – *we may be **products** of our past, but we do not need to be **prisoners** of it.* Man, let me tell you, I cried. This was the first time I had ever heard my father say, "I am proud of you." I would have never heard those words I longed to hear if I had not shown grace.

My childhood was filled with lots of tension, but I have used that all as motivation to be and do what I feel called to. I did not let the tension break me, I allowed it to make me. God put a special part of grace on my life to leverage all of the tensions I have ever experienced, not just in leadership, but also in life.

POISON

The Bible declares, "Look after each other so that none of you fails to receive the grace of God. Watch out that *no poisonous root of bitterness* grows up to trouble you, corrupting many" (Hebrews 12:15 – NLT, *emphasis mine*). The writer of Hebrews was saying that bitterness starts internal but always becomes external. The internal poison of unresolved issues will definitely infect the people around us – ultimately destroying marriages, families, friendships, and churches.

Man, how true is that? Here's the thing: while we are holding on to an issue toward someone, they are going about life! They couldn't care less all while we are holding on to the past. I have met people that live in the past! It is a very sad place to be – they walk around down, defeated, and discouraged. They rain on everyone else's parade because they are living under the pressure of living in the past instead of leveraging the tension. Grace should lead us to leverage the tensions of life and leadership.

There are poisons that cripple the grace in our lives. They surface in multiple places and situations. If we allow these toxic things into our lives, it will keep us from living and leading with grace.

Here are a few:
- **Poison of Frustration** – We take this when we think we are not getting what we earn or deserve. This poison keeps us from celebrating others when they excel!
- **Poison of Insecurity** – Every time we compare ourselves to other people, we take a sip.
- **Poison of Unforgiveness** – This is ingested when we hold on to the past – and refuse to move forward.
- **Poison of Violation** – Someone empties your trust bank by violating some relational boundaries or leadership rules.
- **Poison of The Unresolved** – When you never talk through and resolve the issues that you had to walk through. This not only happens in life, but also in the workplace.
- **Poison of Rejection** – This takes place when facing rejection from an employer, spouse, date or family member and can devastate you.
- **Poison of Abandonment** – Abandonment will cause a level of bitterness that you can never explain. When you feel like every person has or will walk out on you, it will affect every area of your life.
- **Poison of Self-Sabotage** – A lot of times, we continue to hurt ourselves because we refuse or resist to change and then blame everyone else for what we have gone through. We sabotage our lives before someone else can!

What poison have you been drinking? It has an effect. In fact, this affects every single person who is unwilling to address the issues they are facing. For me, I drank the poison of abandonment for too long. I blamed my life and behavior on the absence of my father! Today, I don't cast blame – I offer grace! This has helped my marriage, my parenting, my leadership, and yes, my life!

DOORMAT DOCTRINE

Too many people in life live by what I call The Doormat Doctrine. What is that? It is the willingness to let people walk all over you. Just because you live and lead with grace does not make you a doormat. My mother used to say, "Do you see 'Welcome' written on my forehead? No, then I am not your doormat!" I have lived by that motto for 45 years! No one deserves to be the doormat!

As a leader, there are times when you will have to take it on the chin. There will be moments when you apologize for things that you did not even do. However, there will also be moments when people are abusive, corrosive, and divisive. Don't be the doormat.

When I was growing up in middle school, I faced the dreadful pubescent years. I hated them. I developed really bad acne on my face; especially around my mouth. One of the nicknames that a young lady – who will rename nameless – started calling me was "herpes face." Yep, that's a name every young man wants to be called growing up (I say sarcastically). Not good at all. This caused me to become introverted. It may have just seemed like "kids being kids," but the problem with "kids being kids" is that behavior still has an effect on people. It impacted me.

But something happened my junior year of high school. It was not as much what was happening around me, but what was taking place inside of me. I made a decision. Enough was enough. I was not going to be someone else's doormat. I refused to let anyone walk all over my emotions anymore. I rejected the Doormat Doctrine.

DON'T BE A DOORMAT!

As a person, you cannot allow your life to be marred by those around you. There are people who will live recklessly, but you must still lead with grace. Life has too many great things happening to be blinded by the words of those who show little to no restraint. Yes, grace is giving people more than they deserve, but grace does not mean you allow people to walk all over you!

The tension lies between grace and doormat. How do you really decipher whether or not someone is walking all over you? It could be a co-worker, a spouse, a friend, or even a church member. I think it is pretty simple: *if it is always, only about them, then they are walking all over you.* You see, I have had conversations with people – difficult ones – sharing my perspective as their boss or pastor and I have seen many shift the attention to themselves. "But I need to" or "I felt this way" and they make it all about them. Can we talk about it? Those who make it all about them barely care at all about you!

Doormats are designed to welcome you to someone's home or to wipe your feet off. They are not designed as a template for your life! Don't be the doormat. Don't allow people to trespass on your emotions. Refuse to let others undermine your value. You were not designed to be a doormat.

WHAT ARE YOU FLYING WITH?

How many of you have ever over-packed your luggage for an airplane flight? It's a 50-pound limit and you are at 60 pounds (or more) and they want you to pay an oversized bag fee. Now, what do you typically do? If you have another bag, you might try and balance the weight OR you will throw it into your carry on. That's what we try and do because there is no way I am paying more than I already did. The cost is more than I am willing to pay. Unforgiveness, bitterness, resentment have a larger price tag than we should ever be willing to pay. Grace allows us to empty the luggage of our life that keeps us from experiencing the life God has for us.

What are you flying with today? What excess baggage do you have that you know you should let go of? Every person makes a choice: travel light or travel weighed down. I want to travel light.

Most people never connect forgiveness and leadership, but I believe that strong leaders are able to forgive and move forward. The leaders who cannot own their issues and look through other's issues get stalled. Is there an employee that has hurt you? A parishioner that lied about you? A co-worker that manipulated the facts? You see, every leader knows that you must move forward in spite of all those. But few leaders recognize that forgiveness is the key to moving forward. For me, I knew that I could not just forgive my father, but I had to let him know. It was therapeutic. I did not want to fly with the baggage of unresolved issues!

The Bible declares, "Do all that you can to live in peace with everyone" (Romans 12:14 – NLT). That means that there will be times when you will not be able to resolve conflict. Still, do all that you can! You see, when you do everything possible to travel light, you also lose the guilt for what you could have done or should have done. Whether you fired someone at the office, or you walked away from a friend, ask yourself, "Did I do all that I could?" If you can say yes, then live free of the guilt. That's grace! You see, grace is not just cutting someone else a break. It is also giving yourself a break too!

I have done some stupid things as a person, and as a leader. It's true. But I have had to learn how to give myself some grace. I am very hard on myself. Probably too hard. I watch almost every sermon I preach to evaluate. I review every conversation, every decision, and every meeting. I am constantly trying to get better, but I often feel more discouraged by my self-evaluation than motivated. The problem is, I give more grace to others and less grace to myself.

There will always be things we can do better. No doubt. But let this sink into your leadership think tank: *you cannot fully lead with grace when you live with guilt.* If I was preaching, I would say, "C'mon somebody. That's good." One of the things I have had to come to grips with in the last few years is that I will never be perfect. No matter how hard I try, I will miss out most times. I could always do better at this or that.

Guilt is absent where grace is present! The more grace I give to myself, the more I can then give to others. If I accept the fact that I am not perfect, then it will be easier to accept the reality that others are not either! You are not perfect. That's why you need grace as a human, spouse, parent, child, friend, and leader.

Don't live or lead with guilt. Use grace as your tool. God gave it to you to protect your future. Be filled with grace!

SEVENTY TIMES SEVEN

Peter approaches Jesus and asks, "Lord, how often should I forgive someone who sins against me? Seven times?" (Matthew 18:21 – NLT). Now, this is an out of the blue question. We have no information other than Peter starts this conversation. Jesus' response is simple and profound: "No, not seven times," Jesus replied, "but seventy times seven!" (Matthew 18:22 – NLT). At first this seems like a multiplication problem, but it is really a heart issue. Too many people have tried to do the math on this verse without seeing the real lesson. Jesus is saying that we should give grace to everyone as often as needed.

Jesus was hurt, betrayed, denied, beaten, and murdered by those He came to save. Remember some of His final words: "Father, forgive them!" Without tension, there would have been no need for grace! Tension creates room for us to forgive, extend grace, demonstrate love, and lift people higher. If Jesus can do that while suspended on His cross, then we should be able to do that for those around us too.

I have also discovered the greatest tension of forgiveness is found in forgiving ourselves. That is often the most difficult. We beat ourselves up for our mistakes, failures, and poor choices. Forgive yourself 70 x 7 too. Don't hold on to anything that will hold you back. Forgive yourself. Live free of the guilt. Live in grace. Lead with grace.

As a leader of people, forgiveness is a pre-requisite to leadership. There is no way that you can work with people, lead people, or serve people with a bitter spirit. It will affect every leadership decision you could ever make. Set yourself free.

Forgiveness doesn't just free the person being forgiven, it also free the person offering forgiveness. Live free - forgive. Don't hold on to the pain of the past or the problems you have gone through with people. Let them go. Resist the urge to hold a grudge. Even if you have to forgive someone 70 x 7...

x 7

x 7

x 7

TENSION TIME

Look inside to see what changes can be made outside.

1. What painful moment of your life have you been unwilling to address? Why?

2. Where have you been acting like the "doormat"?

3. Make a list of all the people that you said you forgive, but you never let them know. Then, let them know.

THE POWER OF YOUR POSITION

Leadership is really about understanding your position, your role, or your placement in an organization. Until a leader knows who they are, they will never fully lead like they were created to. Your position is simply your 'status' or 'standing.' It is how you are viewed and by who!

There's a story in the Bible, not well-known, found in the Old Testament book of 2 Chronicles. War breaks out between Abijah and Jeroboam. *Judah*, led by King Abijah, gathered 400,000 warriors. *Israel*, led by Jeroboam, collected 800,000 troops. This battle broke out because Jeroboam rebelled against Solomon's son, Rehoboam. Jeroboam then gathered a group to overthrow this young, inexperienced king. Now the kingdom is divided – North and South, Israel and Judah.

They are now about to go to battle when King Abijah stands on Mount Zemaraim and asks, "Do you really think you can stand against the Kingdom of the Lord that is *led by the descendants of David*? You may have a vast army … but as for us, the Lord is our God, and we have not abandoned Him?" (2 Chronicles 13:8, 10 – NLT, *emphasis mine*). Notice, what the King of Judah declared, "led by the descendants of David." In other words, we know our position! Leaders must know their position. They must know who they are, what they are commissioned to do, and who has empowered them!

An eagle does not hang out with chickens. Why? It knows its position! The eagle does not think to itself, "I would like to be a chicken.' No, it knows who it is and what it is! I have discovered there are many eagle leaders who spend more time with chickens. The result? Insecure leaders! Insecure leaders can never fully manage their position or leverage the tension they face!

One of the things that I have had to learn as a pastor – and this has been one of the toughest – is the principle of distance. As our church has grown, we have had to put some distance between us and the people we lead. Notice, I did not say disconnect, but distance. My wife and I have recognized that our position as pastors can be compromised when people in our church see us as their friends alone. Yes, we have many friends in our church, but we must lead all of our relationships in the context of our position. If we do not, people will place unfair expectations on our family. This has happened many times. These moments have always created tension.

CONFIDENCE OR GODFIDENCE

A dear friend of mine, Buddy Cremeans, is an incredible pastor-leader. He introduced me to this principle of Godfidence many years ago. It has changed my personal narrative. Confidence is the belief you have in yourself, but Godfidence is the belief you have from God about yourself. I wrestle with this tension all the time. I wish I could say that I leverage it 100% in my life, but that would be a flat-out lie!

OUR GOAL IN LIFE AND LEADERSHIP SHOULD BE GODFIDENCE!

As a Christian, I have to embrace the fact that my confidence comes from my position in Christ. It is not based on what I do, what I own, or who I know, but in the call that God has put on my life. My position is secure because I know Whose I am! I am a child of the Most-High God! He created my life and I believe He orchestrates my steps! I can be confident in that reality!

Too many leaders are taught the principles of confidence, but that often turns into cockiness. Talk about tension! Our goal in life and leadership should be Godfidence. Confident about who God made you to be, what God called you to do, and where God wants you to go!

For me, I know who I am. I also know who I am not. I walk in my strengths, but I will never stand on my weaknesses. I recognize that my strengths are gifts from God and my weaknesses remind me of where my strength comes from. In order to lead people, you must know who you are. That's the power of your position!

I love basketball. I love to watch it. I love to play it. To be honest, I am not great, but I can handle my business on the court. As I watch people play pick-up ball, I notice something very quickly – everyone wants the ball! I mean literally every time I play a game. It does not matter if it's the 45-year old overweight guy who thinks he is Steph Curry or the 15-year old that thinks they have handles like Kyrie Irving. Everyone wants the ball. That happens because we have lost sight of the fundamentals of basketball. There are five positions on the court at all times. But everyone wants the one position. When I play, I am ok in my position and role. Partly because my knees can't handle it anymore and I am sucking wind after 5 minutes. Mostly, I play from my position.

The same is true in life. Everyone wants to be in charge until they are. Everyone wants to be the star until they face the criticism. Everyone wants to be wealthy until they see their taxes. However, you can only do or be what God has called you to do or be when you walk in your Godfidence!

I heard Joel Osteen say this to a group of pastors: "Stay in your lane." I have learned that if I stay in my lane, I am less likely to ram someone in the side of their car! If I swerve over the lines, I will inevitably cause a crash! I have to be confident that my lane is where God has called me to be!

EVERYBODY ELSE THINKS

If you desire to lead well and long, you will have to stop living on what everybody else thinks. Now don't get me wrong, there are people in your life whose input matters. What these people say and how they view your decisions should be highly valued. That is not the "everybody" I am talking about. You are going to have a million people who think they can do it better than you can or that always have an opinion for every decision. That's the "everybody" you must stop caring about what they think.

In the beginning of our church, I would catalogue every moment that I prayed for our church. Yes, as I said before, I am a little OCD. It was getting out of control. Eventually I stopped counting, but I catalogued 6,778 hours of prayer for our church. Over the years, this has become a source of protection for our vision. "Pastor, I believe God wants you to do this." My response would be something like, "Have you prayed for 6,778 hours for the direction of our church? If not, start, and when you get to that number you can give me what God has told you." Talk about creating tension. They never came back with their good idea. Here's why: *they were willing to tell you what to do but were not willing to put in the hard-work of prayer*. As a leader, you have to learn to not seek out the approval of those who are not fully in your corner.

STOP FOCUSING ON WHAT EVERYBODY ELSE THINKS.

Church life can be overwhelming and difficult. It is like a revolving door – people come and people go! It's the most difficult part of leadership! I had a conversation with one of the most brilliant pastor-leaders I have ever met, Terry A. Smith. His advice to me was to learn how to *normalize what you experience*. That's just church life. Everyone has an opinion. That's the tough news. Here's the good news: you don't have to agree with it!

I learned many years ago that if you live for the approval of people, you will die for the lack of it. As a leader, you must come to grips with the reality that not everyone is going to like you or what you do. That is okay.

We had someone leave our church. It was painful. We were very close, but they chose to leave. Do you know how they chose to tell us? They texted us! This hurt. No reason given. Just goodbye. Mary and I have had to process it, but we had to learn that we are not going to make everyone happy. In fact, I believe if everyone likes you, then you are probably not doing anything to push people forward. If you want to survive the high speeds of leadership, you will have to stop focusing on what everybody else thinks!

Just to be clear: this does not mean those you trust! Guard your mind and heart from the voices of negativity, those "devil's advocates." There will always be people who need to speak into your life, but not everyone should have that access. This will create natural tension. Leverage it!

GET RID OF THOSE STANCHIONS

One time we received a note on an offering envelope. It was pretty direct. It said, "Get rid of those partitions blocking the seats in the auditorium." It was anonymous. They did not ask us to consider, they simply demanded we change something. I honestly thought for a moment, "Well, at least they could have put something in the offering envelope. I mean, maybe we would have listened a bit more." Kidding (sort of). Needless to say, we did not remove the stanchions.

Most leaders change what they know is right because of the pressure by people. Here's the thing: when you know your position, you don't apologize for walking in it. Leaders lead. They make decisions that upset people. Leadership is about making the tough decisions no one else has the courage to make. They are able to do that because of their position. Leaders walk in that confidence.

So, when someone tells you to get rid of those stanchions or stop doing this or start doing that, hold your position. Don't let people knock you out of your lane. Stay focused. If you know that what you are doing is the right thing, run hard and fast after it. Yes, you will face tension for it, but you will become stronger because of it.

No matter what you face, no matter how many mountains you have to climb, no matter what obstacles you experience, hold your position. There is power in knowing who you are and what God has called you to accomplish. There will be times when you feel crushed, broken, alone, and ignored but hold your position!

THERE ARE NOT ENOUGH DEMONS IN HELL THAT CAN STOP YOU FROM YOUR DESTINY!

You see the enemy of your soul uses opposition to try and get you out of your position, but *your position in Christ is stronger than the opposition of the enemy*! Scripture declares, "… you can be certain that *you belong to God* and have conquered them, for the One who is living in you is far greater than the one who is in the world" (1 John 4:4 – TPT, *emphasis mine*). You belong to God. That is your position! That statement of fact gives you victory over anything and everything! That means, if you are a child of God, you can walk in life and leadership knowing that your position is not found in your titles or achievements, but in your relationship to Christ. That is good news. There are not enough demons in hell that can stop one person who knows who they are in Christ.

When someone tells you to get rid of those stanchions, but you know that they are helpful, don't move them. Stand on your position. Own it. You are called, anointed, equipped, and positioned for the life God has called you to!

THE SELF-CLAP

Singers from the Clan of Korah wrote a poem in Psalm 43. The poem contains a prayer for vindication from false accusations, honest dialogue about discouragement, pain, and at the end they write: *"Then I will say to my soul,* 'Don't be discouraged; don't be disturbed, for I fully expect my Savior-God to break through for me. Then I'll have plenty of reasons to praise Him all over again" (Psalm 43:5 – TPT, *emphasis mine*). Notice what they write, 'Then I will say to my soul …" What are you saying to your soul? What message are you broadcasting to your spirit?

Don't flood your soul with negative self-talk. Don't sip on your own hater-aide. Leaders need to master the art of the self-clap. What is the self-clap? It is when you encourage yourself. You remind yourself that you are talented, gifted, and able to do what God has positioned you to do.

Even when no one is cheering you on, speak to your soul! Get alone in a closet, your bathroom, your office, or your bedroom, and clap yourself to life again. Being in leadership is often lonely and discouraging. That's why you have to speak to your soul.

I am doing better than I thought!

I am God's choice!

I am talented!

I am not crazy!

I am gifted!

I know what I am doing!

I am a winner, champion, and overcomer!

Sometimes you just have to clap yourself to life. If you are an incredible parent, go ahead and clap for yourself. If you are a great teacher or principal, give yourself a clap. If you are a phenomenal athlete… you already hear about how great you are – clap for someone else. Kidding! Give yourself an applause. You are doing better than you give yourself credit for. If the Clan of Korah had to speak to their soul, then so do we! Here's where you must be careful: *watch what you tell yourself!* Make sure that you are honest, but not brutal. Don't fill your mind with negative self-talk, disappointment, and discouragement. The tension of the self-clap rubs against most leaders nature. It seems unnatural.

Clap for me.

Yes, tell your soul what you are good at. Remind yourself that you have skills, expertise, and capabilities. Where did those come from? God! Notice where the Clan of Korah landed. The poem teaches us that after they spoke to their soul, they chose to worship. They redirected their focus on God! When you have a healthy view of yourself, your view of God becomes much clearer.

Now go out and clap for yourself. You know who you are. Celebrate the unique you that God created. When you know who you are, opposition cannot knock you out of your position.

TENSION TIME

Look inside to see what changes can be made outside.

1. List all of your skills, talents, and abilities.

2. What is the hardest thing you face in your position? Why?

3. Find three people and ask them to tell you what they feel are your greatest strengths.

THAT AIN'T OPTIONAL

There are very few things I have ever quit in my life. It may seem like a foreign concept in today's world, but I am pretty loyal. To be brutally honest, I don't like to quit. There are only a few things I have ever walked away from. I did quit McDonald's! Yep. I worked there for 3 hours – not 3 days, 3 weeks, or 3 years – but 3 hours. After my shift ended, I quit. I was young. It was my first job. Not the start I wanted. I was able to rebound. Over the years I have developed this 'Quitting Is Not An Option' attitude.

Now, I like options. In most areas. If you are buying a car you can buy the base model, or you can add some options! Regardless, the steering wheel is not optional, the breaks are not optional, the engine is not optional, the frame is not optional. *Not everything in life is optional*. If you are hitting Baskin Robbins you got 31 flavors, plus all the topping options! Imagine walking into the ice cream shop and saying I want the options without the ice cream. They would think you are crazy! If you go to the hospital and need surgery, they will place you in the operating room. They have all the equipment you need there. But what happens when they send in the janitor in? Excuse me- custodial engineer - to perform the procedure! Let's just put it this way. A doctor ain't optional! You see, *not everything in life is optional*!

Quitting has become the option for many people. They quit on their marriage. They quit on their health. They quit on their church. They quit on their children. They quit on their calling. They quit on their friends. They quit on their leadership. Giving up is the easier solution. You can run away from anything that stresses you out, overwhelms you, or makes you feel uncomfortable. It may seem optional, but it ain't optional.

If you are going to leverage your tensions, you are going to have to quit less. What do I mean by that? You have to quit the things that are holding you back and stop quitting the things that God is using to develop your character and destiny. Just because something causes tension does not give you permission to walk away.

NOT EVERYTHING IN LIFE IS OPTIONAL!

Too many people throw in the white towel of defeat way too early. If you are slow reading this chapter drill down on this moment. God is not done with you yet. Rise from the ground. You may feel bloodied, battered, and broken, but quitting ain't optional!

It seems like every Monday I wake up wanting to quit. In my mind, I have good reasons: attendance was low, giving was down, volunteers were late, no one cares, mad church members, negative conversations. Blah blah blah blah blah. Any person can rationalize quitting, but only the strong leverage their tensions. You see, successful people are not the ones who strike gold the first time around. They are the ones who never give up.

Here's something I have learned: God won't quit on me – so I am not quitting on Him. Refuse to throw in the towel. No matter how hard life gets keep swinging, keep fighting, and keep believing.

Quitting. That ain't optional.

DON'T MAKE EXCUSES

Anyone can make excuses, but not everyone can make a difference. You can make an excuse, or you can make an impact, but you cannot do both. The survivors are the ones who change cultures, impact destinies, and develop winning strategies. Those who leverage their tensions are the ones who people write books about.

"It's too hard."

"You have no idea what I went through."

"It was too much."

"They did this to me."

I am not trying to minimize people's pain, but every person on planet earth has been through some sort of hell. No one is immune to loss, tragedy, or problems. We cannot allow those to become the excuses that keep us imprisoned to self-defeat.

In the beginning, God finishes creating everything! He then tells Adam and Eve that they can eat of anything in the Garden of Eden – except one tree – "The Tree of the Knowledge of Good & Evil." You may know the story – the Serpent comes in and convinces Eve to eat the forbidden fruit. Eve then convinces her husband, Adam. God shows up and He is not happy. He asks Adam, "Have you eaten from the tree whose fruit I commanded you not to eat?" (Genesis 3:11- NLT). His response, "It was the woman you gave me ..." (Genesis 3:12 - NLT). Adam threw his wife under the bus. He did not own it! He made an excuse. It was somebody else's fault. This story gets better. God then asks Eve, "What have you done?" (Genesis 3:13 - NLT). Eve's response, "It was the serpent!" Neither one took responsibility for their actions, they simply made excuses and shifted the blame! Things have not changed today.

People make excuses for everything and anything:

- *I did my homework – but my dog ate it.*
- *I could not go to the game - my wife said "no."*
- *I forgot our anniversary because my boss kept me late.*
- *It ain't my fault – the devil made me do it!*

You and I make excuses all the time about lots of things! I would have fit in those skinny jeans, but I ate 12 brownies. I would have got that promotion, but I never finished my resume. I would have saved all my money, but I bought a mustang, motorcycle, and a boat instead. I would be a great CEO, but all I do is play my Xbox (and I am 45 years old). I would read my bible, but I have to check my likes on Facebook. If we want to become all that God has designed, we have to live an excuse free life.

You see, the reality is you are not defined by your excuses, but by the choices you make! Moses was approached by God through a burning bush. God tells him that he is called to lead God's children out of Egypt to the Promised Land, but Moses says, "No." He makes a list of excuses!

"I am not qualified."

"I don't know enough."

"I don't believe in myself."

"This isn't my calling."

"I am not your guy."

Then God asks him one question, "What is in your hand?" He had his staff and God used that staff. The challenge most people face is wanting someone else's staff. Stick to your staff. What is in your hand? Stop wanting what is in someone else's hand. Don't try and get someone else's gifts, talents, and abilities? Adjust your spiritual life. Adjust your relationships. Adjust your perspective. Adjust your health. Stop making excuses! Start making adjustments!

FIGHT OFF THE DISCOURAGEMENT

I'm not sure how you process decisions or results, but I analyze. Too often I over-analyze. It's true. It is probably not the healthiest thing to do. I go over every detail, moment, conversation, word, and more. I am constantly trying to tweak everything to make it better, but that comes at a price. As a result, I often find when things do not go "as planned" I get easily discouraged.

> **IF THE ENEMY CAN KEEP YOU DOWN,
> HE WILL STOP YOU FROM YOUR DESTINY!**

Even during incredible moments, I can struggle to stay high on hope. The Bible declares, *"he gives his sunlight to both the evil and the good, and he sends rain on the just and the unjust alike"* (Matthew 5:45 - NLT). In other words, everyone faces the good and the bad. No one is immune to times or moments of tension or pressure. Whether you are a preacher, barista, teacher or businessperson you can face the lows of your emotions. There is not one leader who does not battle discouragement from time to time. In fact, I believe if you haven't thought about quitting from time to time, you are probably not trying anything new. Any leader who says, "I never get discouraged," is frankly not being honest or has settled for status quo.

I have learned that if the enemy can keep you down, he will stop you from your destiny. That's why you must fight off the feelings of defeat. God will always bring you through what life has brought you to. Difficulty usually comes in seasons. That means discouragement does too. As a leader, you set the tone. That means you have to work through the discouraging seasons.

Quitting. That ain't optional.

My wife, Mary, and I began our church planting journey over 10 years ago. It has been an incredible ride. We have faced the highs and lows of church planting. I have a friend who planted a church at the same exact time we did. During the same month and same year. Today, they are running three times the size we are. I can easily compare my success with someone else's and become discouraged. To be honest, there are days that I do. I refuse to stay there!

I remember one week feeling so discouraged and I received a call from a great friend, David Crosby. I will never forget what he said. "Todd, God puts the sharpest tools in the hardest soil." Oh man, that was like a shot of caffeine. Planting a church in the Northeast United States is not for the faint of heart. Planting a church in New York Metro is not for the timid. My wife and I chose not to quit. Today, we are so grateful.

KEEP SMILING

Choose to smile. Get your spirit high on hope. Eventually your emotions will catch up. Make the decision that you are going to smile no matter what. Keep your joy high. Focus on all that God is doing right, how He is moving in your life and where He has brought you so far. You are probably doing better than you give yourself credit for.

Certain seasons can be very difficult for leaders. Especially if you are not advancing as quickly as you thought you would. For the first eight years of our church we would post our Christmas and Easter attendances on social media. It was a whole lot of pride! Until I had a conversation with an incredible pastor. He told me that as I was celebrating our success, he was more discouraged because he did not have the same success. In an effort to encourage our church, I didn't realize that I was discouraging another leader. After that conversation, we decided to not post our holiday highs any longer on social media. We now celebrate them in house.

Let me be clear, I have often felt like this pastor too. I can feel like we had a great Easter, until I see someone else's Easter. You cannot get caught up in the comparison trap. It is a dangerous prison that will suck the life out of you and kill your joy. Scripture declares, "The joy of the Lord is your strength," (Nehemiah 8:10 - NLT). Keep your joy high. It will help you leverage your tensions.

SURROUND YOURSELF WITH LIFE-GIVING PEOPLE!

This is huge. Don't miss the next few sentences. I have had to change some of my relationships because they became voices of negativity that robbed my joy. Every conversation I had, it felt like I was drained and exhausted when they were over. Mary and I made the choice to surround ourselves with people who invest into the soil of our lives and leadership! Maybe a few people are coming to your mind right now who are the negative nags. Reduce your time with them and make room for the right people.

Remember leaders, whoever has our ear will have our heart. Be careful who you allow to speak into you. Proverbs 4:3 teaches, "Guard your heart above all else, for it determines the course of your life." Get the right people around you and remove the negative voices. Misery doesn't just love company – it crushes it! Miserable people will crush your dreams, your hopes, your desires, and your spirit. Surround yourself with life-giving people and leaders. Keep smiling.

NEVER QUIT

This is critical. Choose to keep going no matter what. Scripture teaches, *"So let's not get tired of doing what is good. At just the right time **we will reap a harvest of blessing if we don't give up**"* (Galatians 6:9). Stay strong. Keep pushing. You will get where God promised you would be.

My wife and I were facing one of the most discouraging seasons of our ministry. We were gifted a building in Babylon, NY, but it was in bad disrepair. We also inherited a core group of about 8 people. It would be our first attempt at multi-site. Long story short, we invested $150,000 into necessary repairs, but it still needed $200,000 more than we had. All of the remaining 8 had left and we could not get that campus past 25 people. We decided to shut it down and sell the property. In the process, the town revoked our property tax exemption because we were not officially meeting. Fast forward, we ended up selling the property for more than what it was worth. That's how God provided the down payment and renovation finances for the 34,000 square foot former Jewish synagogue we are in today. We say it all the time, "Out of the ashes of Babylon rose Commack."

In the middle of the most discouraging seasons of pastoring, God was doing something behind the scenes that we could not see. We chose to push through what we were experiencing. Mary and I stayed in faith.

We learned to pray more, trust more, and believe more.

One of the enemy's greatest tactics is to get you to quit on your destiny. It is okay to have moments of feeling down, but you cannot stay down. Get up. Trust God. He has a plan and purpose for your life. Scripture promises, "… *God, who began the good work within you, will continue his work until it is finally finished* …" (Philippians 1:6 - NLT).

> **THE ENEMY FIGHTS THE HARDEST THOSE WHO GOD WANTS TO TAKE THE HIGHEST!**

Never forget, the enemy fights the hardest those who God wants to take the highest. Your destiny was hand crafted by God. He will finish what He started. Keep going!

Leverage your tensions!

Never quit!

TENSION TIME

Look inside to see what changes can be made outside.

1. Have you recently thought about quitting? When? Why?

2. How do you overcome discouragement?

3. List the 5 things you never want to quit on.

CLOSING THOUGHT

No matter where you are or what you go through, never surrender to tension. Learn from it. Leverage it. Don't surrender to it. In other words, *don't let tension become your detention*! Refuse to be incarcerated by the things that cause you stress, pain, difficulty, and problems. You see, tension can become a prison, or it can be a platform, but it cannot be both. Choose to lead free. Choose to live free!

I truly believe that God has given every person an anointing to be someone or to do something. That calling comes with tension. I do not believe the best path is always the easiest. Sometimes you have to go through a little difficulty to get to your destiny. There will be times in your life when the stress and tension is so strong that you would rather quit. That's a great place to be! It simply means you are experiencing some tension!

Tension will teach you a lot about life, but even more about yourself. I have learned more about Todd Bishop during the challenging seasons. Tension has a way of revealing who you are! It brings things to the surface that you did not know were there!

For years I battled with insecurity. To be honest, I still do. But you can leverage what causes you tension! I use that insecurity as a motivation. Now, it's not my sole motivator, but it is a little gas in my engine. It keeps me progressing, keeps me working, keeps my striving for more. If I did not wrestle with insecurity, I probably would not be where I am today doing what I am doing!

God uses your tension to move you to a higher dimension. There is no way you will ever grow to a new level without embracing whatever causes you tension. Don't view tension from the perspective that it will hold you back. See it as God's way of preparing you for what lies ahead. Tension becomes a great ally if you choose to allow it to!

As a pastor for nearly 25 years, I have felt the pressure of tension from many different sources. But I have discovered that tension will only stop you when tension becomes your barrier instead of your bridge. I have the deep belief that God uses everything to develop in us the character needed to arrive to that next level.

Someone once said, "For every new level there is a new devil." I am not sure that is always true, but it feels like it many times. Your future as a leader is directly related to how you manage the tension that you experience. No one can escape the tension of life and leadership.

My wife and I experience tension from many levels. Some are easily managed, while others can become very hurtful. We have learned that everything we face in life and leadership is being used to develop our lives. Nothing happens by accident.

Life has not always been easy for me. It seems like that is the case for most people. The difference between successful people and those who just survive is the capacity to use the tension for a greater purpose.

What are you facing today that God is using to reshape and reframe your life and future?

We always stand between choice and choice! "What do you mean?" You see, life is filled with choices. We make decisions all the time. There is not a thing that you do that does not require a choice. Reclining on the couch stuffing your face with Twinkies is a choice. You could have made the decision to get on the treadmill for a 20-minute jog. Choice. You are constantly making choices.

One of the great problems in leadership is replacing choice with excuse. We make excuses for our bad decisions, poor behavior, or negative thoughts. Excuses. I hate them. Over the years I have tried to own every decision I have ever made – good or bad. I choose to own it, not excuse it. Don't make excuses for why your business has stalled or your church is not growing, or your family is falling apart. Own your choices.

The decisions we make in life flow out of our value systems. If you value change, you will constantly evolve as a leader. If you value excellence, you will work towards absolute perfection. If you value time with your family, you will schedule time with your family. Every decision you make in this life is attached to your values.

What decisions do you need to make? In other words, what tension do you need to leverage? Instead of complaining about the struggle – embrace it. Don't allow your tension to become an excuse. Turn it into a choice! Choose to do the right thing right.

So, thank you Chad for inspiring me to write this book. Over the last 15 years I have learned a lot about myself and people through the gift called tension. It's not a gift that I have always enjoyed, but it is one that I have tried to embrace.

Remember, tension is a great teacher. You will discover things about yourself that you did not know when the pressure is turned up! Choose your steps wisely. Focus on what you are called to do.

Never underestimate the power of this one decision: *I will leverage my tensions*!

I WANT TO HEAR FROM YOU

I know that every person has a story. That story matters to them, but it also matters to me. Please feel free to share your story with me. I would love to hear about how God is working in your life or even about the struggles you are experiencing.

I believe that your best days are still in front of you. Keep your eyes on God and He will take you places you could never imagine in your wildest dreams.

To contact me, write to:

Todd Bishop
83 Shirley Court
Commack, NY 11725

Or email me: todd@toddbishop.tv

You can also visit my website, www.toddbishop.tv, for inspirational readings and blogs.

  @toddrbishop

ABOUT THE AUTHOR

Todd Bishop is a dynamic communicator with a passion to reach those who are far from God, while inspiring the found to go find more. He is a leader of leaders who consistently devotes himself to building the local church! Todd is a creative leader with the capacity to present the complexities of God's Word in a simple way. He is a strong champion for the lost, the broken, and the forgotten.

Todd serves as Lead Pastor of CHURCH UNLEASHED, along with Mary, his wife, which they started in 2008. They have one goal – plunder Hell and populate Heaven. Their God-sized vision is to change the culture of Long Island, NY and beyond.

In 2009, Todd was recognized by the Assemblies of God as one of their 25 Groundbreaking Church Planters. He was also honored during the 2009 General Council of the Assemblies of God with an Award of Excellence for his work in Church Planting. Todd was also awarded the distinction of "Young Alumni of the Year" from his Alma Mater, Central Bible College, in 2010.

In 2014, Hicksville, New York showered Todd and Church Unleashed with numerous awards and citations for the work that they have been doing in the city. Community, civic, religious, and political leaders from the area have recognized Todd's love for Long Island.

In 2015, Todd received the prestigious "Empowering Long Island Award" at Madison Square Garden from the Empowerment Summit Committee. This award was given to recognize Todd's incredible work in the non-profit sector that has helped empower people to become all that they are designed to be.

Todd authored his freshman book, "The Human Right," in 2018. New York Times bestselling author Mark Batterson says, "Todd Bishop is the real deal, and it comes through in *The Human Right*. The down-to-earth, yet uplifting truths found in these pages will inspire you to be you." In 2019, Todd is releases his new book, "Leveraging Tension," a book that encourages you to not allow tension to knock you out of commission. Ed Young Jr believes, "*Leveraging Tension* is full of practical tools for growing through trials and adversity so that you can become the leader God destined you to be!"

Todd is a sought-after speaker for conferences, leadership gatherings, and church services. His relevant approach to life and leadership make him approachable and understandable!

Todd & Mary live on Long Island, NY with their three amazing children, Malachi, Abigayl and Bethany.

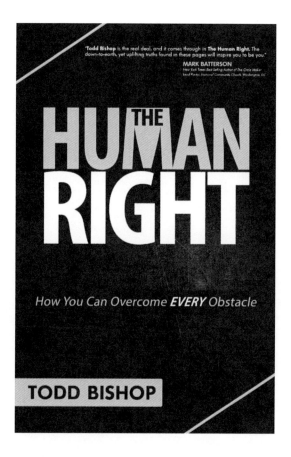

In **The Human Right**, Pastor Todd Bishop shares the ten rights that every person has been given by God. He shares many life stories and draws principles from God's Word. If you have ever faced challenges or are in the thick of difficulty, Todd will inspire you to never give up and to keep dreaming.